Mark practised in major commercial law firms for thirty years, special-ising in property dispute resolution. He has acted for businesses large and small, including FTSE-listed property companies and household-name corporate occupiers, across the whole range of property-related issues. He has wide experience in conducting contentious applications for consent, and advising upon lease variations.

He is now a full-time commercial property management law trainer, putting his expertise and experience to good use in training both lawyers and surveyors. He delivers training for providers including MBL Seminars, Central Law Training, Professional Conferences, CPT Events and Solicitors Group.

Mark is also the author of The Lease Guide website (www.theleaseguide.co.uk), which aims to provide helpful and practical guidance in an understandable and digestible format to small businesses taking a lease.

A Practical Guide to Applications for Landlord's Consent and Variation of Leases

A Practical Guide to Applications for Landlord's Consent and Variation of Leases

Mark Shelton

MA (Hons) Law (Cantab), Non-Practising Solicitor

Commercial Property Management Law Trainer

Author of The Lease Guide website

www.marksheltontraining.co.uk

www.theleaseguide.co.uk

Law Brief Publishing

Published 2018 by Law Brief Publishing, an imprint of Law Brief Publishing Ltd
30 The Parks
Minehead
Somerset
TA24 8BT

www.lawbriefpublishing.com

Paperback: 978-1-911035-92-3

PREFACE

This book is concerned with the mechanism by which landlords exercise control over what tenants may do upon a property. This is usually done by providing that certain things may only be done with the landlord's prior consent. The process of obtaining consent (if the tenant), and considering, often resisting, the grant of consent (if the landlord), is a recurring flashpoint in the landlord-tenant relationship. Moreover, it can throw up tricky technical issues, so some practical guidance through the process is essential.

In principle, when a property is leased, it is the tenant's to do with as it wishes during the lease term. In the case of a long residential lease, granted perhaps for a 999-year term at a peppercorn rent, the landlord has, to all intents and purposes, disposed of the property completely, and one would expect it to have only minimal control over what the tenant does.

In the case of a typical commercial lease, however, granted for a term possibly as short as six months, and seldom for a term longer than 40 years, the landlord retains a significant interest in the property. It will be mindful of the fate of the property after expiry of the lease term, and will want to have it back in a condition that keeps open all options as to reletting, selling or perhaps redevelopment. In other words, it wants to preserve the value of its investment. It is a priority that the tenant in occupation should be of sufficient financial substance to comply with its obligations as to payment of rent, and the repair and insurance of the property. Equally, the landlord will be concerned to limit the permitted business uses of the property, as well as what alterations may be made to it.

On the tenant's part, it will want freedom to deal with the property in whatever way it considers most beneficial to its commercial activities. That may simply be a matter of what sort of business it is permitted to conduct at the property; it may be a matter of reconfiguring the property, or installing specific facilities or equipment; or it may be a matter of disposing of the property, if it has become surplus to requirements or uneconomic to run.

The objectives of landlord and tenant will not necessarily conflict, but the lease drafting must anticipate the possibility that they will, and the usual means of providing for that is to prohibit certain actions by the tenant, unless the landlord gives its prior consent to any such action. A combination of drafting convention, contractual interpretation by the courts and legislative activity has restricted the scope of the landlord's discretion as to the giving or refusing of consent, and this simple issue of whether a landlord can be brought to say 'yes' has given rise to a significant body of law and practice.

While the law on this topic does not generally differ as between residential and non-residential properties, the typical content of the restrictions contained in a residential lease is different from that of the restrictions in a lease of commercial property. As observed above, a long residential lease is likely to have very little in the way of restriction. In the more common case of a short-term residential tenancy at a market rent, alterations to the property are likely to be absolutely prohibited, and the only permitted use will be residential, while if the tenant wishes to be rid of the property, the usual way out is by giving notice to terminate the tenancy, rather than assigning the lease or sub-letting. It follows that, in the absence of any provision for the landlord to consent to alterations, assignment, sub-letting or change of use, the law relating to landlord's consents can have no application. It is therefore in the commercial context that most of the caselaw has arisen. This book will focus on landlord's consents in the context of commercial leases.

It is not infrequently the case that the tenant seeks consent to some action which is simply prohibited, without any provision in the lease for the landlord to consent to it. The landlord may be minded to allow the action regardless, and if so, the landlord's 'consent' is in reality a variation of the lease. That may be recognised by the parties, in which case the documentation of the matter will take the form not of a simple licence deed, but of a deed of licence and variation. There are formalities and best practices to be observed in relation to such express lease variations. Sometimes, the parties will not have realised that they are varying the lease, and the documentation will simply take the form of a licence deed. This can be problematic. This book addresses issues arising from lease variations as well.

In a commercial law firm, the documenting of landlord's consents and lease variations is referred to generically as 'lease management', and is often allocated to junior fee-earners or perhaps to legal executives or paralegals, in order to keep costs down. That reflects the perception of clients that such matters are routine administrative procedures, and should be dealt with quickly and cheaply. However, they can give rise to really difficult problems, which can expose clients to significant financial consequences. It is hoped that this book helps both to identify and to avoid the problems.

The law is stated as at 31 August 2018.

Mark Shelton
September 2018

CONTENTS

CHAPTER ONE
TYPICAL CONTENT AND EFFECT
OF LEASE RESTRICTIONS

This chapter considers the usual content and effect of lease restrictions placed upon tenants in relation to alienation, alterations and change of use. It refers to relevant parts of the *Code for Leasing Business Premises in England and Wales*, and introduces the *Alienation Protocol* and the *Alterations Protocol*. It also outlines relevant considerations when more than one type of application for consent is made at the same time.

Types of prohibitions in leases

If a lease makes no provision in relation to a particular action which the tenant proposes to carry out upon the premises, then in general the tenant has a right to go ahead with that action, and does not require any consent from the landlord. It is only if that action is prohibited by the terms of the lease that landlord's consent becomes a relevant requirement. Prohibitions fall into different classes. The classic analysis is that prohibitions imposed upon tenants in leases may be absolute, qualified or fully qualified.

- An absolute prohibition does not contemplate any consent by the landlord, but simply bans the action outright. That is not to say that the landlord may not be persuaded to consent to the prohibited action regardless, however such a 'consent' would in reality amount to a variation of the lease terms. The landlord's discretion as to whether to grant or refuse consent in such a case is absolute.

- Under a qualified prohibition, the action may not be undertaken unless the landlord gives its prior consent.

- Under a fully qualified prohibition, the action may not be under-taken unless the landlord gives its prior consent, not to be unreasonably withheld. The usual form of words is 'not to be unreasonably withheld or delayed', but where the words 'or delayed' are omitted, a sufficiently lengthy delay can of course amount to 'withholding'. The effect at common law of a fully qualified prohibition is considered in the next chapter.

Absolute and fully qualified prohibitions are routinely encountered in leases, when dealing with the main areas of restriction: alienation, alterations and use. Qualified prohibitions are rare.

Typical restrictions

Alienation

'Alienation' simply means dealings with the leased property. One thinks immediately and naturally of assignment of the lease, and sub-letting, but restrictions are usually much broader in scope.

Clauses typically begin with a very broad prohibition of assignment, sub-letting, charging, holding on trust, and parting with or sharing possession or occupation. This prohibition usually applies both in relation to the whole of the premises, and in relation to part of them, and will be expressed as an absolute prohibition. However, it will be subject to exceptions as provided for in the remainder of the clause.

- There will generally be an exception permitting assignment of the lease as a whole, with the landlord's prior consent, not to be unreasonably withheld or delayed. There may be specific circum-stances set out in the clause in which the landlord will be entitled to refuse consent (for example the proposed assignee does not meet some financial test), or conditions which the landlord will be entitled to impose upon any consent (for example provision by the proposed assignee of an acceptable guarantee). Assignment of part of a lease, while theoretically possible, gives rise to difficult technical and practical problems, and so is usually not within the scope of this exception; it is therefore absolutely prohibited.

- Sub-letting is usually dealt with in some detail, and whether sub-letting of part is permitted will depend largely upon the nature of the property. A tenant whose lease comprises five floors of an office block may well be permitted to sub-let individual floors (sometimes half-floors, depending on the configuration of the building). A tenant of a light industrial unit, on the other hand, will probably not be permitted to sub-let in part, since the property may not be easily divided.

Insofar as sub-letting is permitted, whether in whole or in part, there are usually pre-conditions: typically, a proposed sub-letting may only be allowed by way of exception to the general absolute prohibition if: (a) it is to be at the best market rent obtainable; (b) it is to be otherwise upon all the same terms as the lease; and (c) it is to be contracted out of the *Landlord and Tenant Act 1954*. Provided all those pre-conditions are met, sub-letting is permitted with the landlord's prior consent, not to be unreasonably withheld or delayed.

- There are sometimes arrangements for groups of companies, whereby sub-letting to companies within the same group as the tenant is permitted, without any requirement for a specific consent. Parting with or sharing occupation or possession is sometimes also permitted to group companies, again without any specific consent.

As to occupation and possession, to a layman they may be inter-changeable expressions, but in law they are different. The distinction between possession and occupation in the context of alienation restrictions was considered at length in *Akici v L R Butlin [2006] 2 All ER 872.*

The *Code for Leasing Business Premises in England and Wales 2007* recommends that where landlord's consent to an assignment or sub-letting is required, it should be provided that consent is not to be unreasonably withheld or delayed. In other words, the prohibition in the lease should be in the fully qualified form. While the Code is not binding, s.*19(1), Landlord and Tenant Act 1927* applies to transform any qualified prohibition on assignment or sub-letting into a fully qualified one (this provision will be considered more fully in the next chapter). The combined effect is to make it rare to see an alienation restriction in the qualified form. It will be either absolute or fully qualified.

In certain circumstances, it may be very important to landlords to have complete control over dealings with the property. In some retail leases, for example, rent is calculated by reference to the tenant's turnover. A proposed assignee's business model may be very different from that of the incumbent tenant, and the amount of rent that the landlord would receive could be reduced if the lease were to be assigned. Rather than have its decision submitted to a reasonableness test in the courts, the landlord will wish to have absolute discretion.

One answer to that is to make the prohibition absolute, though this may be commercially unacceptable to the tenant, and would have an adverse impact upon valuation in any rent review. The alternative is to include an 'offer-back' provision: a requirement that prior to making an application for consent to assign or sub-let, the tenant must first offer to surrender the lease to the landlord. The landlord then has the option to bring the lease to an end by accepting the offer, rather than submit to the reasonableness requirement.

Such provisions may also be used where high rental growth is anticipated, so that instead of the tenant assigning the lease for a premium, the landlord can re-let at a higher rent.

Doubt was thrown on the effectiveness of such provisions by the decision in *Allnatt London Properties Ltd v Newton (1983) 45 P. & C.R. 94*, in which the agreement to surrender was held to be unenforceable under *s.38(1), Landlord and Tenant Act 1954*. While in theory that consequence could be avoided by following the procedure under *s.38A* of the 1954 Act for contracting-out the surrender agreement, in practice there was no way of compelling the tenant to do so. It is now thought, following the reforms to the 1954 Act which came into effect on 1 June 2004, that an effective offer-back procedure is possible (though this has never been tested in the courts) and some leases provide for this.

Alterations

When looking at an alterations covenant in a lease, it may be relevant to bear in mind the broader commercial context. In *Bickmore v Dimmer [1903] 1 Ch 158*, the tenant fixed a large clock on the outside of the premises, by means of bolts which went six inches into the wall, to advertise its business of selling watches. This was held not to fall foul of the prohibition on alterations, since the parties must have contemplated that a tenant would carry out acts which would be usual in the conduct of its business. That is an old case, and it would be usual now to see express provision dealing with external facia and advertisements, but it is a reminder that it is always necessary to consider the meaning and extent of the restriction.

The wording of the alterations covenant will depend upon the type of building and the extent of the demise. A lease of whole will typically permit the tenant to carry out a broader range of alterations than a lease of part. In a lease of part, structural and external works are often not permitted at all, and this is sometimes the case with a lease of whole. A tenant of a stand-alone industrial unit will expect to have more flexibility than a tenant of a unit in a shopping centre. Different landlords have different policies as well.

These different outcomes are achieved by distinguishing between different categories of alteration.

- Certain types of work may not be prohibited at all, being specifically permitted by a blanket permission in the lease. A lease of office premises, for example, might permit the installation and removal of demountable partitioning, while a warehouse lease might permit the installation and removal of full-height racking. Sometimes the permission is expressed more broadly, to allow any internal non-structural work. So long as the tenant's proposed work falls within this category, specific consent is not required, although there is normally a covenant to notify the landlord after the works have been carried out.

- At the other end of the spectrum, there is generally a category of work which is absolutely prohibited. This is likely to include structural work, and may perhaps extend to matters affecting the external appearance of the property. That may be important where the building is listed, or is in a conservation area, or simply for maintaining the visual unity of a development. Since the prohibition is absolute, the law relating to landlord's consents is irrelevant, though as mentioned above it may be that the landlord will be persuaded to consent to work of this nature, the 'consent' taking the form of a variation to the lease.

- It is the third, residual category which is of interest in the context of the issues addressed in this book: alterations subject to a fully qualified prohibition. Work in this category can only be carried out with the landlord's prior consent, not to be unreasonably withheld or delayed.

It would be unusual to encounter a proposed alteration which was not provided for in one of the different categories. In that rare situation, though, a landlord may have a fall-back protection, in the law of waste. The law relating to waste is archaic, and is rarely of practical significance. 'Voluntary waste' means damaging the premises by some deliberate or negligent act, and may provide a remedy in the case of alterations which are not controlled by the lease. Liability for voluntary waste arises in tort independently of what the lease may say, but it is often addressed in the tenant's lease covenants as well.

The *Code for Leasing Business Premises in England and Wales* recommends that:

- A landlord's control over alterations should be no more restrictive than necessary to protect the value of the landlord's property

- Internal non-structural alterations should be permitted without any requirement for landlord's consent, unless there will be an impact on services and systems in the wider building

<u>Use</u>

The use clause (or 'user clause') in a lease sets out the permitted use of the property. Older leases very often also contained a lengthy list of objectionable uses which were specifically prohibited, and these lists tended to have a long and not very distinguished history, with further prohibited uses being added into lease precedents on an *ad hoc* basis over the years, while nobody thought (or perhaps dared) to remove out-of-date items. A clause might prohibit use of the premises for various archaic business types, such as those of a blood-boiler or tallow-chandler, for example, while a more contemporary addition might be use for the purposes of a social security office or unemployment exchange.

Modern leases rarely contain that sort of list, and instead generally confine themselves to identifying the permitted use, and prohibiting all other uses. There is generally also a restriction on any use which may cause nuisance or annoyance to neighbouring occupiers, which presumably deals with those pariahs the blood-boilers and tallow-chandlers, and some leases specifically prohibit use for illegal or immoral purposes.

The prohibition on all but the permitted use is generally an absolute one, so that questions of landlord's consent rarely arise. Retail leases, though, may contain a fully qualified, or sometimes just a qualified, prohibition. A lease might provide for a specific use such as the sale of ladies' fashion clothing, while permitting any other retail use with landlord's consent, not to be unreasonably withheld or delayed. In such a case, a change to anything other than another retail use would fall within the absolute prohibition.

It is unusual for a dispute over change of use to turn upon a reasonableness provision in the user clause, however. More commonly, where a retail tenant proposes to assign or sub-let, and the incoming third party requires a change of use, the relevant clause of the lease is the alienation clause, since the caselaw establishes that the intended use of the premises by an assignee or sub-tenant may justify refusal of consent to the assignment or sub-letting.

Planning controls

There will normally be a separate covenant governing whether the tenant is permitted to make planning applications, which may be needed before tenants can make alterations or change the use of premises. The landlord will be concerned that a breach of planning law by the tenant could lead to enforcement action against the landlord, and potentially have an adverse impact on the investment value of the property.

Usually the lease will provide that the tenant will not apply for, or implement, a planning consent without the landlord's consent, not to be unreasonably withheld or delayed where the landlord has consented to the activity underlying the tenant's application for planning consent (i.e. alterations or change of use). There may also be a provision that if the tenant implements a planning consent, it will comply with any conditions, and implement the consent in full, before the end of the term. The landlord's concern is that if the tenant leaves a consent only partly implemented, the local authority could require the landlord to complete the implementation after the lease has ended.

As regards use, the permitted use of the property will fall within one of the Use Classes set out in the *Town and Country Planning (Use Classes) Order 1987*, and indeed the user clause may well define the permitted use by reference to one or more such Use Class. Change from one Use Class to another generally requires planning permission, though some shifts between Use Classes are permitted by the *Town and Country Planning (General Permitted Development) (England) Order 2015.*

It is important to bear in mind that the two restrictions, contractual and statutory, are parallel and unconnected. If a change of use from one Use Class to another is permitted by the planning legislation, it may still be prohibited by the use clause in the lease, and the planning position will not necessarily determine whether a landlord's refusal to permit change of use is reasonable or not.

Combined applications

As suggested above, a proposal to assign a lease, or to sub-let, may well be accompanied by a proposal to change the use of the property. Even more likely is that the incoming occupier will wish to make some physical changes to the property, so that there may be a need to obtain the landlord's consent to alterations as well. If the alterations or change of use require planning consent, that restriction is engaged too, so that four separate consents may be required for one transaction.

This may have implications as regards the degree of control which the landlord can exercise. As we shall see, the landlord may be in difficulties in refusing consent to an assignment or sub-letting, but may be on much firmer ground in refusing consent to alterations. If the alterations are an integral part of the transaction, then that is a back-door route to a much greater degree of control over the assignment or sub-letting. This factor can also have consequences for the tenant's ability to recover damages for an unreasonable refusal by the landlord. We shall return to these considerations later.

Protocols

Although this chapter is not concerned with matters of procedure, it is convenient to make early mention of two protocols which give useful guidance on applications for landlord's consent. The website www.propertyprotocols.co.uk has been established as a joint enterprise between the law firm Hogan Lovells LLP and Falcon Chambers, one of the leading sets of barristers' chambers practising in landlord and tenant matters. It has published a small (so far) number of protocols which aim to assist in avoiding property disputes, or if unavoidable, resolving them.

The first one published was the *Protocol for Applications for Consent to Assign and Sub-let*, abbreviated to the *Alienation Protocol*. The second was the *Protocol for Applications for Consent to Carry Out Alterations*, or the *Alterations Protocol*. They can be downloaded free from the website, together with accompanying explanatory materials.

Neither is in any way binding, nor is there yet any suggestion of them having been quoted in court as being persuasive. However, their provenance is excellent, and the content is soundly based upon the existing law and best practice. While these documents are not, accordingly, controversial, they do include some practical suggestions whose widespread adoption would be welcome. At the very least they can be regarded as a form of useful checklist for dealing with such applications, whether acting for landlord or for tenant.

They are mentioned here because the procedures outlined in them follow from the legal analysis of different types of prohibition, and from the nature of the statutory interventions in this field, and because they contain commentary on factors likely to be of relevance in assessing reasonableness. All these matters are the subject of the next few chapters, and it will be useful to refer to relevant parts of the Protocols as we proceed.

Summary

There are three types of prohibitions in leases governing tenant's activities upon the premises: absolute, qualified and fully qualified. It is unusual to see a qualified prohibition; they are usually either absolute or fully qualified.

As regards alienation, leases usually contain an absolute prohibition on any dealings with the property, in the widest terms, but subject to detailed exceptions. The exceptions will usually include a fully qualified prohibition on assignment of the lease as a whole, so that the lease may be assigned with the landlord's consent, not to be unreasonably withheld. A further exception will often be a fully qualified prohibition on sub-letting. Each is typically subject to further detailed control in the terms of the lease. There is sometimes also a provision permitting intra-group assignments or sharing arrangements, again usually subject to restrictions. 'Offer-back' clauses may be included where control is particularly important to the landlord, so that the landlord may elect to accept a surrender of the lease rather than permit the tenant to make an application for consent to assignment or subletting.

Alterations covenants usually separate types of work into different categories:

- Those permitted generally, without any need for specific consent.

- Those prohibited absolutely, such as structural works.

- Those subject to a fully qualified prohibition, which may therefore be carried out with landlord's consent, not to be unreasonably withheld.

It is only the third category which raises any issues of landlord's consent.

Change of use is generally subject to an absolute prohibition, though retail leases may have an exception by means of a fully qualified prohibition, permitting change to another retail use with landlord's consent, not to be unreasonably withheld.

Landlord's consent may also be required in relation to making planning applications, and this is usually on a fully qualified basis, so that landlord's consent may not be unreasonably withheld.

It is often the case that more than one type of application is made together, and this may have tactical implications as to the degree of control which the landlord can in practice exercise.

Two protocols, the *Alienation Protocol* and the *Alterations Protocol*, contain useful procedural and substantive guidance in this area of law and practice.

CHAPTER TWO
STATUTORY INTERVENTIONS

This chapter summarises the legislation relevant to landlord's consents: *s.19(1) – 19(3) Landlord and Tenant Act 1927*, the *Landlord and Tenant Act 1988*, and the *Landlord and Tenant (Covenants) Act 1995*. It also considers the effect at common law of a proviso that landlord's consent is not to be unreasonably withheld, and the extent to which landlords may prescribe what is reasonable by means of provisions in the lease.

The wording of the lease is not the only consideration when trying to ascertain the scope of the tenant's freedom of action, and the extent of the control which the landlord is able to exercise. There has been significant legislative activity in this area, starting with *s.19(1) – 19(3), Landlord and Tenant Act 1927*.

s.19(1), Landlord and Tenant Act 1927 – alienation

s.19(1) deals with assignment and sub-letting (also charging and parting with possession), and provides in effect that where a lease contains a qualified prohibition, it is converted into a fully qualified prohibition. In other words, where landlord's consent is required, a proviso is implied into the lease to the effect that landlord's consent must not be unreasonably withheld.

Effect of fully qualified prohibition at common law

It may be natural to assume that where that proviso applies, either by express agreement or by reason of the operation of *s.19(1)*, a landlord who is found to have acted unreasonably in withholding consent will potentially be liable to pay damages to the tenant. However, in *Rendall v Roberts & Stacey (1959) 175 EG 265*, a tenant's claim for damages was dismissed, on the basis that there was no actual covenant by the landlord not to unreasonably withhold consent, merely a proviso which qualified the general wording of the phrase in which it appeared.

In an earlier case, *Ideal Film Renting Co, Ltd v Nielsen [1921] 1 Ch 575*, damages had been awarded. The lease in that case contained a substantive covenant by the landlord not to withhold consent unreasonably. The following remarks by the judge in *Ideal Film Renting* were quoted with approval in *Rendall v Roberts & Stacey*:

> "*It is established beyond controversy that if the covenant on the part of the lessee not to assign without consent is merely qualified by a proviso that the consent of the lessor is not to be unreasonably withheld, there is no implied covenant by the lessor that he will not unreasonably withhold his consent, and in the absence of an express covenant to that effect no action will lie against him for unreasonably withholding it. But even so the lessee is not left wholly without remedy, for if in fact the consent is unreasonably withheld he can effectually assign without consent.*"

The function of a proviso of this type, therefore, is this: if (a) a tenant seeks consent to do something which requires landlord's consent; (b) the landlord unreasonably refuses it; and (c) the tenant then goes ahead and does it anyway, the presence of the proviso establishes that there is no breach of covenant on the tenant's part. It affords a defence, not a cause of action. Alternatively, a tenant might, rather than simply proceeding without consent, apply to court for a declaration that the withholding of consent was unreasonable.

That is the common law position, but as regards alienation it has been modified by the *Landlord and Tenant Act 1988*. The common law position still applies, though, in relation to applications for landlord's consent to carry out alterations to the premises, or to change use (so long as the prohibition on change of use is a fully qualified one).

Landlord and Tenant Act 1988

Prior to 1988, then, the law relating to consent to alienation assisted tenants to a certain degree, but the assistance was limited. For a tenant wishing to offload premises and bring its rental commitment to an end, progressing the transaction would have been a matter of priority; for a landlord or its agent, the application for consent was more likely to appear as a rather boring piece of routine administration, which may only have received attention after more interesting and lucrative matters had been dealt with: completing a new letting, perhaps, or settling a rent review. If the landlord was either deliberately obstructive, or persisted in some objection which the tenant considered plainly unreasonable, there was little effective remedy. Proceeding without landlord's consent would be risky, and by the time a declaration had been obtained from the court (also a risky enterprise, of course) the prospective assignee or sub-tenant might well have found other premises, and abandoned the transaction. The *Landlord and Tenant Act 1988* addressed these issues.

Where the lease contains a qualification to the effect that landlord's consent to an assignment, sub-letting, charging or parting with possession is not to be unreasonably withheld, then *s.1* of the 1988 Act is engaged, with the result that the landlord is under a number of duties:

- to give consent unless it is reasonable not to do so;

- if imposing conditions upon a grant of consent, only to impose reasonable ones;

- when refusing consent, to give its reasons for doing so;

- when imposing conditions, to stipulate what the conditions are; and

- to give its decision in writing within a reasonable time.

Breach of any of the statutory duties entitles the tenant to claim damages under *s.4*. For good measure, *s.1(6)* also reversed the burden of proof. At common law (*International Drilling Fluids v Louisville Investments (Uxbridge) [1986] Ch. 513*) it was for the tenant to demonstrate that the landlord had been unreasonable; now it is for the landlord to prove that it has been reasonable.

The 1988 Act therefore made a major change to the balance of power in these situations. It is the key piece of legislation in relation to alienation consents. It does not apply to alterations applications, and not directly to change of use applications, though proposed user is a matter which may affect the landlord's response to an alienation application.

Landlord and Tenant (Covenants) Act 1995

A restriction requiring landlords to act reasonably involves, of course, a degree of uncertainty, since opinions may differ as to what is reasonable or unreasonable. Alienation clauses in leases are therefore usually drafted so as to attempt to regain some control, and impose greater certainty as to what is or is not reasonable. The law does not obstruct this objective to any great degree, though market practice is that tight control is rarely acceptable.

Prescribing what is reasonable in the lease

In *Re Smith's Lease, Smith v Richards [1951] TLR 254* it was held that provisions stipulating circumstances in which a landlord's refusal of consent will be reasonable are of no effect:

> "*the parties cannot restrict the ambit of s 19 by stipulating expressly that this or that shall be deemed to be reasonable. The question is objective: Is it reasonable? That question has to be decided without regard to the interpretation which the parties have put on that expression.*"

However, according to *Adler v Upper Grosvenor Street Investments [1957] 1 WLR 227* and *Bocardo v S&M Hotels [1980] 1 WLR 17*, provisions which operate as conditions precedent to the ability to assign, sub-let or perform some other action requiring landlord's consent, are effective. It is only when the condition precedent has been satisfied that any question of the landlord's reasonableness falls to be considered.

Therefore: (a) a provision stating that it would be reasonable for a landlord to refuse consent to a sub-letting which was not contracted-out of the *Landlord and Tenant Act 1954* would be ineffective; but (b) a provision stating that a tenant might sub-let with landlord's consent, not to be unreasonably withheld, but only on condition that the sub-lease would be contracted-out, would be effective.

The distinction is, as the courts have recognised, a semantic one, and on which side of the line any particular provision falls is a question of construction. It would be unusual, however, for such a restriction to be drafted sufficiently carelessly as to suggest an attempt to prescribe what is reasonable, rather than the imposition of a condition precedent.

Landlords can, therefore, exercise control by means of conditions precedent.

The 1995 amendments to the Landlord and Tenant Act 1927

Further help for landlords in this respect came with the *Landlord and Tenant (Covenants) Act 1995*. *s.22* of the 1995 Act amended the 1927 Act by inserting new sub-sections, *s.19(1A) – (1E)*. The reason to legislate was that the 1995 Act abolished the old scheme of privity of contract, as it applied to leasehold covenants.

To explain briefly: a tenant who takes a lease usually covenants to pay the rent, and to observe and perform all the other tenant's covenants in the lease, throughout the term. Should the lease be assigned, the assignee usually covenants in the licence to assign to the same effect, and this will happen on all assignments throughout the term.

Under the law prior to the 1995 Act, this meant that once a tenant or assignee had assigned the lease, and therefore ceased to be liable through privity of estate (i.e. by virtue of their status as tenant for the time being), they nevertheless retained liability by virtue of their contractual obligations. In this way, each time the lease was assigned, the landlord added another name to the list of those liable to pay the rent, and perform the other tenant's covenants. One consequence of that was that landlords could be relatively relaxed about assignments.

The effect of the 1995 Act is that from 1 January 1996, in relation to most leases granted post-1995, the assigning tenant is automatically released from liability on the lease covenants. This happens immediately upon the assignment. By way of exception to the general principle of release, the landlord may be entitled to require that they enter into an Authorised Guarantee Agreement, or 'AGA'. That is an agreement by which an assignor guarantees performance by their assignee of the tenant's covenants, but that liability as guarantor ceases upon any further assignment. In other words, a tenant's liability in relation to the lease covenants can only be extended, beyond their time as tenant, for the period during which the lease remains vested in their immediate assignee, and not any subsequent assignee. (This limitation to the immediate assignee's tenure does not reflect any coherent principle, but is simply a pragmatic compromise between the competing interests of landlord and tenant). That means that the contractual liability of tenants is lost, as the lease goes on and is subject to successive assign-ments. It follows that landlords are much more concerned about controlling assignments, and *s.19(1A) – (1E)* were inserted into the 1927 Act in recognition of that.

s.19(1A) – (1E) apply only to post-1995 leases. They provide that where landlord and tenant have agreed circumstances in which consent to an assignment may be withheld, or conditions which the landlord may impose upon grant of consent to an assignment, then a landlord who refuses consent in those circumstances (provided they exist), or who imposes those conditions, shall not be regarded as acting unreasonably. The agreement may be contained in the lease or in some separate doc-ument, and it may be made at the same time as the lease or at some other time, so long as it was prior to the application for consent being made.

There is what should be regarded as an anti-avoidance measure, which is the only restriction upon the content of any such agreement. Under *s.19(1C)*, if the circumstances or conditions it identifies are framed by reference to a determination of some matter by the landlord (or by any other person), then either the agreement must provide that the power to make the determination must be exercised reasonably, or there must be provision for independent review of the determination. Otherwise, the provision that the landlord shall not be regarded as acting unreasonably does not apply.

The sum effect of these provisions is to make it possible, only as regards consent to assignments, for landlords to prescribe what is reasonable, though not in so many words.

Common s.19(1A) provisions

Most commercial leases contain so-called 's.19(1A) provisions'. When the 1995 Act was new, a considerable amount of ink was spilled in drafting provisions to take advantage of *s.19(1A)*, however as mentioned above the market has generally rejected too tight a control by the landlord.

- There is likely to be a provision entitling the landlord to impose a condition that an outgoing tenant should enter into an Authorised Guarantee Agreement. Under *s.16*, an AGA is only permitted and effective, by way of exception to the general automatic release of the assignor, where it is entered into pursuant to a condition lawfully imposed upon the grant of consent by the landlord. That may mean a condition imposed pursuant to a s.19(1A) provision, or it may simply be a condition which it is reasonable in the circumstances for the landlord to impose pursuant to *s.19(1), 1927 Act*, and *s.1, 1988 Act*.

Where there is a s.19(1A) provision entitling the landlord to impose this condition, the *Code for Leasing Business Premises in England and Wales 2007* suggests that it should be limited so that an AGA can only be required "where reasonable". In *Wallis Fashion Group Ltd v CGU Life Assurance Ltd [2000] 2 EGLR 49 Ch D*, a lease granted prior to 1995 came up for renewal under the 1954 Act, and there was dispute over what new alienation provisions should be included in the new lease to reflect the change in the law. The court held that there should be a s.19(1A) provision entitling the landlord to require an AGA, but that it should be limited by the words "*where reasonable*". Nevertheless, it is common to encounter provisions where the requirement is not limited in that way.

- There may be s.19(1A) provisions entitling the landlord to refuse consent if the proposed assignee fails to meet some financial test. Purely arithmetical accounting tests are not much in favour, since they may fail to take into account significant matters such as contingent liabilities, and insofar as they are typically based upon analysis of filed accounts, they can only reflect a snapshot of the proposed assignee's financial position at the accounting date. They tend therefore to be poor predictors of the assignee's ability to perform the lease covenants. Sometimes the test is that the financial substance of the assignee, together with that of any guarantor, is at least equal to that of the assigning tenant; major occupiers will find that unacceptably restrictive, and in any event it may be hard to assess whether or not the test is satisfied, at least without the input of a forensic accountant.

- It is increasingly common to find provision that assignment to the current tenant's guarantor can be refused. This is as a result of caselaw concerning the operation of the 1995 Act, to which we shall return.

- There is likely also to be provision entitling the landlord to require a rent deposit in a specified amount, or the provision of an acceptable guarantor (additional to any AGA), or both. This would usually be limited by 'where reasonable' wording, and therefore adds little to the position under statute and caselaw.

s.19(2), Landlord and Tenant Act 1927 – alterations

s.19(2) of the 1927 Act deals with prohibitions on carrying out improvements. The relevant lease restriction will invariably use the word 'alterations', and while any improvement must also be an alteration; it does not follow that all alterations are improvements. However, what amounts to an improvement is looked at from the tenant's point of view (*Lambert v Woolworth & Co [1938] Ch 883*), and presumably the reason why a tenant wishes to alter a property will be to increase its usefulness for the purposes of their business; certainly they are unlikely to be intending the opposite. It is therefore hard to imagine any alteration which a tenant proposes which will not be an improvement for the purpose of *s.19(2)*. The landlord will have in mind the prospects for re-letting at the end of the term, and will not consider a proposed alteration to be an improvement if it seems likely to damage those prospects. Nevertheless, that is not a relevant consideration for *s.19(2)*, though it has relevance to other aspects of the statutory scheme under the 1927 Act. *s.19(2)* expressly contemplates that an 'improvement' may not add to the letting value of the property.

The effect of *s.19(2)*, like *s.19(1)*, is to convert a qualified prohibition into a fully qualified prohibition: the requirement for consent is deemed to be subject to a proviso that landlord's consent cannot be unreasonably withheld. As observed in the previous chapter, it is accordingly rare to see a lease which contains a qualified prohibition – usually it will be either absolute or fully qualified.

The *Landlord and Tenant Act 1988* does not apply to prohibitions on alterations or improvements. Possibly the rationale is that in the case of alienation, the tenant risks the loss of the deal with the third party if the landlord behaves unreasonably, while there is no such risk as regards alterations. Where there is a proviso for the landlord to act reasonably, accordingly, it is not a positive obligation; in this regard the law concerning improvements is where the law regarding alienation consents was prior to the 1988 Act. A landlord who acts unreasonably will not be liable to pay damages.

As foreshadowed in the previous chapter, this may mean that a landlord actually has more control over assignment or sub-letting than seems to be the case, since an application for consent to assign or sub-let is often accompanied by an application for consent to alter. A retail assignee may often need consent to assignment, alterations and change of use. The landlord may remove any risk of exposure to damages under the 1988 Act by consenting to the assignment, while maintaining objections to the alterations and change of use. Even if those objections are unreasonable, the landlord does not risk having to pay damages; moreover, the burden of proof is on the tenant to show that the landlord has been unreasonable. There is no duty on the landlord to make a decision on alterations or change of use within a reasonable time, so no risk to the landlord in delaying. In practice the alterations for which consent is sought frequently include some element of works outside the demise, or subject to an absolute prohibition, and in either case reasonableness is irrelevant: the landlord is entitled to say no for any reason or none. If the alterations are sufficiently important to the assignee, the landlord's refusal will actually prevent the assignment, but at no risk of liability to pay damages.

The reasonableness requirement imposed by *s.19(2)* expressly does not prevent the landlord from requiring as a condition of giving consent:

- payment of a reasonable sum for any damage to or diminution in the value of the landlord's property (including any neighbouring property);

- payment of any proper legal or other expenses of dealing with the application for consent; and

- an obligation on the tenant, if it is reasonable to require such an obligation, to reinstate the property at the end of the term, so long as the improvement does not add to the letting value of the property.

The *Code for Leasing Business Premises in England and Wales 2007* recommends that reinstatement at the end of the term should only be required where reasonable, and the landlord should notify the tenant that it is required to reinstate at least six months before the end of the term.

s.19(3), Landlord and Tenant Act 1927 – change of use

s.19(3) of the 1927 Act deals with use restrictions, but its effect is much more limited than that of *s.19(1)* or *s.19(2)*. It provides that where the lease contains a qualified prohibition, the landlord cannot charge a 'fine' (i.e. a capital sum or rental equivalent) as a condition of granting consent (so long as the change of use does not involve any structural alteration of the premises). However, as in the case of improvements, the landlord can require:

- payment of a reasonable sum for any damage to or diminution in the value of the landlord's property (including any neighbouring property); and

- payment of any proper legal or other expenses of dealing with the application for consent.

In the absence of any express proviso in the lease that landlord's consent to a change of use is not to be unreasonably withheld or delayed, there is no deemed or implied statutory requirement for reasonableness. There is little caselaw, therefore, dealing with whether or not a landlord has acted unreasonably in relation to a request for consent to change of use. Where use has featured in the caselaw is in relation to alienation consents, since the assignee or sub-tenant's proposed use of the premises may well be a ground for the landlord to refuse consent to the transaction, whether or not the user clause says anything about landlord's consent or reasonableness.

In the event that there is an express proviso that landlord's consent to change of use is not to be unreasonably withheld, the common law position applies: there is no claim for damages if in fact the landlord unreasonably withholds consent.

Summary

s.19(1) of the *Landlord and Tenant Act 1927* applies to alienation restrictions which require landlord's consent, and deems them to be subject to a proviso that consent is not to be unreasonably withheld. *s.19(2)* makes equivalent provision in relation to restrictions on alterations.

The proviso does not, however, entitle a tenant to claim damages if the landlord does unreasonably withhold consent. As regards alienation restrictions, however, damages are available to the tenant in the event that the landlord breaches any of the statutory duties set out in *s.1, Landlord and Tenant Act 1988*:

- to give consent unless it is reasonable not to do so;

- if imposing conditions upon a grant of consent, only to impose reasonable ones;

- when refusing consent, to give its reasons for doing so;

- when imposing conditions, to stipulate what the conditions are; and

- to give its decision in writing within a reasonable time.

At common law any provision in the lease purporting to prescribe what would be reasonable or not would be ineffective. Landlords can nevertheless tighten their control by a combination of (a) conditions precedent to the ability to assign the lease, or to perform other actions requiring landlord's consent, and (b) provisions taking advantage of the power conferred by *s.19(1A) – (1)(E)* of the *Landlord and Tenant Act 1927* (inserted by the *Landlord and Tenant (Covenants) Act 1995*). The latter power applies only as regards assignments of the lease. It enables provisions in the lease which prescribe (i) circumstances in which the landlord shall be entitled to refuse consent, and (ii) conditions which the landlord may impose upon any grant of consent.

s.19(3) of the 1927 Act provides that where change of use requires landlord's consent, the landlord may not require a payment as the price of consenting.

CHAPTER THREE
REASONABLENESS – GENERAL PRINCIPLES

This chapter considers the general principles governing the assessment of whether or not a landlord has been unreasonable in refusing consent, or in imposing conditions upon a grant of consent. It discusses: how to identify what is a 'collateral advantage'; a landlord may be reasonable without being right; where the detriment to the tenant of a refusal is disproportionate to the benefit to the landlord; and the limitation on the ability to refuse consent to alterations where the landlord could instead require payment of compensation for damage to the property.

The outcome of the conventional drafting practices and the legislation outlined in the previous two chapters may be summarised as follows:

- If a specific proposed action by the tenant falls within an absolute prohibition, then a landlord has unfettered discretion whether to agree to it, and is not subject to any requirement not to be unreasonable.

- If there are conditions precedent which must be satisfied, in order for the specific proposed action to fall within a fully qualified prohibition rather than an absolute one, then no reasonableness requirement arises unless and until those conditions precedent have been fulfilled.

- As regards assignment of the lease, the parties may in effect agree certain responses by the landlord which cannot be considered unreasonable.

- Subject to those three points, landlord's consent to assignment, sub-letting, or alterations may not be unreasonably withheld. This may also be the case as regards change of use, but only if the lease so provides.

The question whether the landlord's position is reasonable is therefore usually at the heart of any dispute arising from an application for landlord's consent.

The accretion of caselaw concerned with decisions as to whether landlords have acted reasonably has led clients and their agents routinely to seek legal advice as to whether a decision, an objection or a condition is reasonable. That is perhaps inevitable, but is a slightly unhappy state of affairs. The point of using the word 'reasonable' is to enlist the common-sense commercial judgment of business people, and it is often salutary to use that as a sense-check, rather than relying exclusively on decided cases.

Decided cases, after all, are simply decisions as to what a court considered reasonable or unreasonable in the context of specific leases, and specific sets of circumstances. Few of the cases purport to lay down general principles, and by and large they do not therefore operate as precedents in the strict sense. A decided case tells you what *was* reasonable on one occasion, as a factual matter, rather than what *is* reasonable for all time, as a matter of law.

That said, the body of caselaw is substantial, and contains a great deal of illumination as to what may be considered reasonable or otherwise, and why. Indeed, this and the next two chapters are occupied in discussion of it. As we shall see, a perfectly proper and sensible commercial objection, which is 'reasonable' in a colloquial sense, may not be 'reasonable' in the sense which the law employs in dealing with these questions. While it is therefore necessary to be familiar with the caselaw, the better approach to it is to focus on the general principles.

Alienation

As regards alienation, the starting-point in considering whether a landlord's refusal or conditions are reasonable is *International Drilling Fluids v Louisville Investments (Uxbridge) [1986] Ch. 513*. This is the leading case, and is one of a small number which do purport to lay down guidance of general application. It concerned a proposed assignment, but the principles laid down in it have wider application, to all types of alienation, and to other consents as well. (There are certain specific considerations in relation to sub-letting, which will be dealt with in chapter 6).

Balcombe LJ delivered the leading judgment in the case, and he stated seven principles. It is the first two which are the most important.

Principle 1 – Purpose of the restriction

- The purpose of the restriction in the lease is to protect the landlord from having its premises used or occupied in an undesirable way, or by an undesirable tenant or assignee.

This principle identifies the sort of matter with which the landlord may properly be concerned: the characteristics of the third party, and the use to which the premises are proposed to be put. 'Use' here encompasses a broad range of considerations: not just the type of business, but also its style and the assignee/sub-tenant's business model.

Principle 2 – No collateral advantage

- As a corollary to that, a landlord is not entitled to refuse his consent on grounds which have nothing whatever to do with the relationship of landlord and tenant in regard to the subject matter of the lease.

It will normally be reasonable for a landlord to refuse consent or impose a condition if this is necessary to prevent his contractual rights under the lease from being prejudiced by the proposed assignment or sub-lease. It will not normally be reasonable for a landlord to seek to impose a condition which is designed to increase or enhance the rights that he enjoys under the lease.

An example of such a 'collateral advantage' arose in *BRS Northern Ltd v Templeheights Ltd [1998] 2 EGLR 182*, in which a tenant wished to assign its lease to Safeway Stores Ltd, for use as a superstore. The landlord was negotiating the development of a neighbouring site as a Sainsbury's superstore, and was naturally concerned that the assignment to Safeway would prevent that scheme from going ahead. Nevertheless, the alienation covenants were not designed to protect the development value of neighbouring land, and to try to use them to do so was to seek to have a greater degree of control than the lease envisaged: a collateral advantage.

Equally in *Allied Dunbar v Homebase Ltd [2002] EWCA Civ 666*, the landlord objected to the rental level of a proposed sub-letting, which would be unhelpful evidence for rent review purposes. The alienation covenants were not intended to assist the landlord in maintaining a false rental market, and to do so would be a collateral advantage.

These examples illustrate that commercial common-sense, on its own, does not tell you what is 'reasonable'. Any property investor would recognise that the landlords' objections to the proposed transactions in those two cases reflected entirely sensible, even obvious, commercial concerns. Determining whether a landlord's objection was 'reasonable', in the special sense intended in this context, requires the legal analysis of identifying the purpose of the covenant, and asking whether the landlord's objection fell within the areas of concern at which the covenant was addressed.

That is the key to determining whether or not the landlord is trying to secure some 'collateral advantage', which is not always easy, though it is a crucial question. Another recent example may assist:

Hautford Ltd v Rotrust Nominees Ltd [2018] EWCA Civ 765 concerned a six-storey building which was let on a 100-year lease. The lease permitted the whole of the building to be used for retail, office and residential purposes. There was a high degree of flexibility, so that no particular part of the building was designated for any specific one of those uses. However, the building had planning permission for retail use on the first two floors, office use on the middle two floors and residential use on the top two floors.

Previously the tenant had tried to acquire the freehold by enfranchisement, but this was successfully opposed as only 25% of the building was used for residential accommodation. The tenant subsequently converted the middle two storeys into flats and sub-let them to residential occupiers, all of which was permitted under the lease. What was not permitted under the lease was making an application for planning permission without landlord's consent, and the tenant needed planning permission to change the use of the middle two storeys to residential. Landlord's consent was not to be unreasonably withheld.

A request for landlord's consent was made, which the landlord refused on the grounds that such a change of use would enhance the tenant's ability to acquire the freehold by enfranchisement. The landlord cited a number of cases where it had been held to be reasonable for landlords to refuse consent because of a likelihood of successful enfranchisement.

The Court decided, though, that the landlord had acted unreasonably in this instance. Unlike the position in the previous authorities cited by the landlord, the lease had been granted after the enfranchisement legislation had been introduced; if the landlord had been concerned to prevent enfranchisement, that could and should have been addressed expressly when the lease was being negotiated. The purpose of the restriction on making planning applications was to protect the landlord from enforcement action by the planning authority. The landlord could not use it to achieve the collateral advantage of preventing part of the building being used for a purpose already expressly authorised elsewhere in the lease.

The issue of collateral advantage is discussed further below, in the context of alterations, and in particular in relation to situations where the landlord trades from an adjoining or neighbouring property, in which case additional considerations may apply (to alienation as well as to alterations).

Principle 3 – Burden of proof

• The onus of proving that consent has been unreasonably withheld is on the tenant.

As mentioned earlier, this rule has now been statutorily reversed where *s.1, Landlord and Tenant Act 1988* applies.

Principle 4 – Reasonable, not right

• It is not necessary for the landlord to prove that the conclusions which led him to refuse consent were justified, if they were conclusions which might be reached by a reasonable man in the circumstances.

In *Norwich Union Life and Pensions v Linpac Mouldings Ltd [2009] EWHC 1602 (Ch)*, the lease contained a tenant's break option that was personal to Linpac. Linpac assigned the lease to a group company, with landlord's consent, so that the break option fell away. Subsequently the tenant sought consent for a re-assignment back to Linpac, and the landlord refused on the basis that this would in effect revive the break option. The High Court concluded that once a lease containing a personal break option had been assigned away from the party with the benefit of the break, that had the effect that the break option fell away for good, and a re-assignment back to that party would not revive it. The landlord was, therefore, wrong in law; nevertheless, it was a legitimate concern, plainly to do with the relationship of landlord and tenant in regard to the subject matter of the lease, and not an attempt to obtain a collateral advantage. The legal point was not obvious, and in the circumstances the landlord had not acted unreasonably in withholding consent.

When advising landlord clients, they may well be nervous about maintaining an objection to a proposed transaction if they cannot show, to a high degree of proof, that their objection is justified. As the *Norwich Union v Linpac* case shows, they can often afford to be more robust. So long as a reasonable landlord could have held the same view, they are not being unreasonable.

Principle 5 – Proposed use

- It may be reasonable for the landlord to refuse his consent on the ground of the purpose for which the proposed assignee or sub-tenant intends to use the premises, even though that purpose is not forbidden by the lease.

As previously mentioned, a modern lease is unlikely to contain a long list of prohibited uses. However, should the tenant propose to assign or sub-let to a tallow-chandler or blood-boiler, the absence of a specific prohibition of those uses does not prevent the landlord from objecting on the grounds of (presumably) objectionable smells, which might be a nuisance to neighbouring occupiers.

It is this principle which allows a court to consider the suitability of a proposed use as part of the assessment of whether the landlord has been reasonable in objecting to the transaction. Hence, most cases concerning consent to change of use are decided by reference to the lease's alienation restrictions, rather than by reference to any fully qualified prohibition on change of use.

Principle 6 – Disproportionate detriment

- While a landlord need usually only consider its own interests, there may be cases where there is such a disproportion between the benefit to the landlord and the detriment to the tenant, if the landlord withholds his consent to an assignment, as to make it unreasonable for the landlord to refuse consent.

This was an important factor in the decision in *International Drilling Fluids* itself. The landlord's objection to the proposed assignment was essentially that if it were to go ahead, the value of the landlord's reversionary interest would be adversely affected. The court found that there was no prospect of the landlord realising the value of its interest by selling it or mortgaging it during the term, and that the alleged diminution in value was therefore only a paper loss. On the other hand, the tenant had already vacated the premises, and remained liable on the tenant's covenants, and the disadvantage it would suffer if the assignment were prevented would be serious.

The 'disproportionate detriment' argument has featured in several reported cases since, but has rarely succeeded.

<u>Principle 7 – A question of fact</u>

- Subject to all those propositions, it is in each case a question of fact, depending on all the circumstances, whether the landlord's consent to an assignment is being unreasonably withheld.

This is hardly a surprising observation; it applies to all questions of reasonableness. It is, though, a useful check on the tendency to elevate decisions in this area into principles of law.

The *International Drilling Fluids* principles have stood the test of time, and continue to form the basis of decisions on reasonableness in relation to alienation.

Alterations

The wider applicability of the *International Drilling Fluids* principles is illustrated by *Iqbal v Thakrar [2004] EWCA Civ 592*, in which the court adapted those basic principles to the context of alterations.

<u>Principle 1 – Purpose of the restriction</u>

- The purpose of the covenant is to protect the landlord from the tenant carrying out alterations and additions that could damage the landlord's property interests.

Principle 2 – No collateral advantage

- A landlord cannot refuse consent on grounds that are unrelated to its property interests.

As in *International Drilling Fluids*, these two principles set out the scope of what the landlord may and may not properly take into account. They do not quite tell the whole story, though.

In *Sargeant v Macepark (Whittlebury) Ltd [2004] EWHC 1333*, the landlords ran a golf and country club, which hosted social function activities such as wedding receptions. Their premises adjoined that of their tenant, whose permitted use was as a hotel, conference centre, management training centre, and fitness and health complex. The tenant asked for consent to build an extension with ten syndicate rooms and a conference hall capable of accommodating 700 people. The landlords were concerned about potential competition from the hotel as extended, and granted consent subject to a condition that the use of public rooms in the extension would be limited to management training conference activities. The tenant challenged the condition as being unreasonable.

Among the issues in the case was the question whether or not the landlord could properly take into account the risk of damage to its trading interests, as opposed to its property interests. The court considered that in circumstances where the landlord traded from adjoining or neighbouring premises, it was permissible to take this factor into account.

In coming to that conclusion, the court referred to *Sportoffer Ltd v Erewash Borough Council [1999] 3 EGLR 136*, in which the landlords were the local authority, and operated an adjoining swimming pool complex. The tenants ran a squash club and applied for consent to alterations and also change of use, proposing to convert some of the squash courts into a leisure-type swimming pool. The landlords objected on the ground that the proposed change would damage the viability of their own complex; and their refusal was upheld as reasonable by Lloyd J.

Similar considerations have arisen in relation to alienation as well. In *Whiteminster Estates Ltd v Hodges Menswear Ltd [1974] EGD 324*, the landlords carried on business as men's outfitters. They also owned the shop next door which had been let as a café. The tenant applied for consent to assign the lease to another men's outfitter, and the landlord refused on the ground that the proposed assignee would be a direct competitor. Pennycuick V-C held that the landlords' fear of an adverse effect on their trade was one that could reasonably be held. He continued:

> "*Once it was accepted, as now it must be, that a landlord was entitled to take into account his own interests as well as his interests as a landlord, that was really an end of the matter. It was sufficient that the landlord could reasonably anticipate that the opening of the new shop would prejudice his trade.*"

It appears, therefore, that it is stating the position a little too narrowly to say that a landlord may only take into account its property interests. Trading interests may also be taken into account, although this appears to be of application only where the landlord occupies and trades from neighbouring premises. A contrast with *BRS Northern v Templeheights* (referred to earlier in the discussion of collateral advantage in the alienation context) perhaps indicates a demarcation line: in that case, the landlord's objection that the assignment would damage the *development value* of the neighbouring site was not a permissible consideration.

Principle 3 – Burden of proof

- It is for the tenant to show that the landlord has unreasonably withheld consent.

Since the *Landlord and Tenant Act 1988* does not apply, this statement remains accurate in the alterations context.

The tenant cannot discharge this burden unless it has made sufficiently clear what its proposals are, in order to enable the landlord to make an informed decision. In *Iqbal v Thakrar* itself, the landlord objected to the proposed alterations on the basis of concerns as to the structural impact upon the property. The tenant had failed to provide sufficient information on the proposed works for the landlord to be aware of precisely what the impact on the structure would be, and it could not therefore discharge the burden of proving that the landlord had acted unreasonably.

A useful contrast is provided by another case decided in the same year, *Shapiro v Mayhew (01.11.04, Central London County Court)*. There, the parties jointly owned the freehold of a house divided into two flats, each of them having a lease of a flat on one floor. In effect, therefore, each party was the other's landlord, and under the terms of the leases, either of the two tenants would require their neighbour's consent to carrying out alterations to their flat. The claimant, who was tenant of the upper flat, requested permission to convert the loft, and the defendant refused on the ground that the claimant had not considered the impact this would have on the structure of the building.

Applying *Iqbal*, the judge nevertheless came to the opposite result, namely that no reasonable landlord could have refused consent. This was because of a very different factual situation. The lessee had provided sketches of the proposed works and had indicated that building regulations approval had been obtained. The landlord had not sought any advice before refusing consent, and had simply raised an unspecific concern as to the structural impact.

Although the tenant succeeded in *Shapiro v Mayhew*, this principle, that it is for the tenant to show that the landlord has been unreasonable, is another of the factors which gives landlords a higher degree of control over applications for consent to alterations than they enjoy over applications for consent to alienation, where the opposite rule applies.

Principle 4 – Reasonable, not right

- It is not necessary for the landlord to prove that the conclusions which led it to refuse consent were justified if they were conclusions that might have been reached by a reasonable landlord in the particular circumstances.

Principle 5 – Proposed use

- It may be reasonable for the landlord to refuse consent to an alteration or addition to be made for the purpose of converting the premises for a proposed use, even if the use is not specifically prohibited by the lease. But whether such refusal is reasonable or unreasonable depends on all the circumstances.

An example of an unreasonable objection on the basis of use is provided by *Iqbal v Thakrar* itself: the proposed use was a permitted use and the intention of the tenant in acquiring the premises to use them for that purpose was known to the landlord when it acquired the reversion.

Principle 6 – Disproportionate detriment

- There might be cases where it would be disproportionate for the landlord to refuse consent, having regard to the effects upon it and the tenant.

It has been suggested earlier that this principle seldom assists tenants very much in practice. An example is provided by *Dulwich Estate v Baptiste [2007] EWHC Ch 410*, in which the landlord refused permission for loft conversion works on the basis that the proposed dormer window did not comply with relevant management guidelines governing the Dulwich Estate.

The issue was the impact of the refusal upon the tenant. As there was no evidence that there was any actual necessity for the loft conversion, but there was evidence that the conversion could still be built without the window, the landlord was entitled to refuse consent. The preservation of the visual unity and amenity of the estate were important objectives, and it was not disproportionate to make decisions so as to preserve them.

Principle 7 – Objection solely on pecuniary loss

- Consent cannot be refused on the basis of pecuniary loss alone. The proper course in this situation is for the landlord to ask for a compensatory payment.

This is a departure from the *International Drilling Fluids* template, and it follows from the wording of *s.19(2), Landlord and Tenant Act 1927*. It may be recalled that the reasonableness requirement imposed by *s.19(2)* is subject to certain 'carve-outs'. One is that it does not prevent the landlord from requiring, as a condition of giving consent, the payment of a reasonable sum for any damage to or diminution in the value of the landlord's property (including any neighbouring property). It was held in *Lambert v Woolworth & Co [1938] Ch 883* that a landlord who had not sought to impose such a condition, but had instead simply refused consent, had acted unreasonably. A well-advised landlord, therefore, if concerned about damage to or diminution in the value of its property, will not refuse consent, but will grant it on condition of a compensation payment. If unsure about the level of the sum demanded, or if the amount is disputed, it can (as suggested in *Lambert v Woolworth*) offer to abide by an arbitrator's decision.

In *Sargeant v Macepark*, it was argued that the landlords' concern as to adverse impact on their trading interests was a matter of pure pecuniary loss, and that accordingly they should have granted consent on condition of a compensatory payment. However, the court took the view that it was not the alterations themselves that had the potential to damage the landlords' business interests, but the use that the tenant might make of the alterations. That approach effectively restricts the ambit of the requirement to grant consent, on condition of a compensatory payment, to circumstances in which it is the *property* (or neighbouring property owned by the landlord) which will be damaged or diminished in value by the proposed alterations, rather than any other matter capable of being assessed in monetary terms.

It will not always be easy to identify the extent to which this carve-out from *s.19(2)* interferes with the landlord's discretion to refuse consent. In *Iqbal v Thakrar*, in response to the landlord's concerns as to the structural impact of the works, the tenant argued (unsuccessfully, because of their failure to provide sufficient information) that the landlord should have granted consent, conditional on the tenant ensuring that the alterations were carried out without causing structural problems. A possible alternative approach might have been that the landlord's objection was really founded upon 'damage to the property', and that consent should therefore have been granted upon condition of a compensation payment. If a landlord fears that his building will be at risk of collapse as a result of the tenant's actions, can Parliament really have intended that he should not be able to refuse consent, but only to require compensation? It is an unattractive proposition, but the on the wording of *s.19(2)* it is not unarguable.

Principle 7 – A question of fact

- In each case it will be a question of fact, dependent on the particular circumstances of the case.

Summary

Most of the caselaw concerning whether or not a landlord has acted reasonably consists of assessments on specific sets of facts, and does not lay down general principles.

In the context of alienation, the leading case which does establish general principles is *International Drilling Fluids v Louisville Investments [1986]*, and the important principles which emerge from it are:

- Landlords can properly be concerned with the characteristics of a proposed assignee or sub-lessee, and the use which it is proposed they will make of the premises.

- Landlords cannot properly seek to obtain a 'collateral advantage' by using the alienation covenants so as to exercise a degree of control over other matters which goes beyond the purpose of the alienation restrictions.

- A landlord can sometimes be considered to have been reasonable even in circumstances where it can be shown that it was mistaken in the conclusions which led it to its decision on the application for consent.

- The proposed use of the premises may still be a valid objection even where it is not specifically prohibited by the lease.

- If the detriment to the tenant of a refusal is disproportionate to the benefit the landlord will gain from it, that may make the refusal unreasonable.

As regards alterations, the case of *Iqbal v Thakrar* lays down the general approach, adopting and adapting the *International Drilling Fluids* principles. Distinctive further aspects of the approach to alterations are:

- A landlord may generally only take into account the effect of the proposed alterations upon its property interests, although where the landlord trades from adjoining property, its trading interests can also be legitimately considered.

- It is for the tenant to prove that the landlord has been unreasonable, not (as is the case in relation to alienation) for the landlord to prove that it has been reasonable.

- Consent cannot be refused where the objection is that the alterations will cause damage to the property (or the landlord's other neighbouring property), or diminution in value. Instead the landlord should grant consent on condition that the tenant pays compensation.

CHAPTER FOUR

REASONABLENESS – COMMON ISSUES

This chapter addresses specific issues which have recurred in the caselaw when courts have been required to decide whether or not a landlord has been reasonable. They include: a requirement for the tenant to pay the landlord's legal and other costs; the position where a landlord relies upon some matters which are considered to be reasonable, and some which are not; the need to obtain superior landlord's consent; adverse impact upon the value of the landlord's interest; unlawful discrimination; breaches of tenant's covenants; and a risk of leasehold enfranchisement.

As a reminder of the status of the caselaw in this area, it is hard to better this extract from the judgment of Lord Denning MR in *Bickel v Duke of Westminster [1977] 1 QB 517*:

> "*The landlord has to exercise his judgment in all sorts of circumstances. It is impossible for him, or for the courts, to envisage them all... Seeing that the circumstances are infinitely various, it is impossible to formulate strict rules as to how a landlord should exercise his power of refusal. The utmost that the courts can do is to give guidance to those who have to consider the problem. As one decision follows another, people will get to know the likely result in any given set of circumstances. But no one decision will be a binding precedent as a strict rule of law. The reasons given by the judges are to be treated as propositions of good sense - in relation to the particular case - rather than propositions of law applicable to all cases.*"

In deciding whether a landlord has been reasonable or not, there are issues which recur repeatedly. The caselaw thus identifies various 'given sets of circumstances' in which a 'likely result' can be anticipated. In this chapter we consider some of these issues, being those which have relevance to all types of application for landlord's consent. In the next two we shall look at other recurring issues which are specific to the alienation context.

Costs

Landlords routinely require payment of their legal and surveyor's costs in relation to dealing with requests for consent, and this can be very contentious.

If you sell your home, you are unlikely to need anyone's permission to do so, and the requirement for consent to an assignment or sub-letting of a commercial property can seem to tenants to be an imposition. Having to pay the landlord's lawyers for the privilege is rubbing salt into the wound, and of course tenants tend to regard the level of costs typically demanded as too high, and particularly so if the tenant's solicitors are a smaller provincial practice, while the landlord uses a major commercial firm in London.

From the landlord's point of view, though, the tenant is effectively asking a favour – it wants to do something which requires the landlord's co-operation. The landlord is likely to regard it as absolutely normal and reasonable that it should have its fees paid, in those circumstances.

Plus, the transaction may well be one which has serious implications for the landlord. An assignment may threaten to dilute the covenant strength; an underletting raises the prospect of a third party, which the landlord has not previously approved, going into occupation of the landlord's property; alterations to the property, or changes of use, can have a knock-on effect upon value, or upon relations with neighbouring occupiers, who may also be the landlord's tenants. The landlord will want to scrutinise the transaction carefully, and to have the benefit of legal advice on its position.

As to the work done for the fee, tenants may be inclined to think that the landlord's solicitors do little more than send out a standard form document, and agree a few minor amendments. In reality, advice on the potential implications is likely to be required, as well as advice on the reasonableness of what the landlord would like to do or say. This is going to involve detailed instructions, and consideration of the title deeds and the legal context.

Whatever the rights and wrongs, costs are a familiar flashpoint when dealing with applications for landlord's consent.

In legal terms it is generally considered to be reasonable for a landlord to require a solicitors' undertaking that the costs of the application for consent will be paid. Both sides were agreed on this in the case of *Dong Bang Minerva (UK) Ltd v Davina Ltd [1996] 2 EGLR 31*, which meant that the Court did not have to rule on it – however, the members of the Court of Appeal said nothing to throw doubt on the position.

That case concerned a lease which expressly provided that the tenant should pay the landlord's reasonable costs in relation to a request for consent to a dealing with the property. Where the lease contains no such provision, it has nevertheless been held in *Holding and Management (Solitaire) Ltd v Norton [2012] UKUT 1 (LC)* that this was still a reasonable requirement.

An alternative to a solicitor's undertaking is for there to be an actual upfront payment of costs on account.

As to the level of the costs, the *Dong Bang* case decided that it was unreasonable for the landlords to require a full indemnity for their costs, whatever the amount. The tenant's solicitors had offered an undertaking to be responsible for the landlord's reasonable costs, and the Court held that it was unreasonable for the landlord to have tried to insist on something more stringent.

Tenants may therefore resist a requirement for an undertaking in relation to a stated figure, if it is thought to be excessive, and insist on giving instead an undertaking for the landlord's reasonable costs. This is a two-edged sword, though, since the reasonable figure might eventually exceed the figure originally quoted.

Other than offering an undertaking limited to reasonable costs, tenants may of course seek to persuade the landlord to accept an undertaking for a lesser figure than that put forward by the landlord, or to agree a cap on costs. However, it is the tenant who is typically under time pressure to get on with the transaction for which consent is needed, and so the negotiating position is not a strong one, particularly where the *Landlord and Tenant Act 1988* does not apply, so that the landlord has no exposure to a claim for damages.

The most direct approach to the problem is to challenge directly the reasonableness of the landlord's costs condition, as in *Dong Bang*, though of course this involves litigation risk. Courts may incline to sympathy towards tenants in relation to this issue. The case of *No 1 West India Quay (Residential) Ltd v East Tower Apartments Ltd [2016] EWHC 2438 (Ch)* turned largely on costs in the end, and the court took the view that the landlord had failed to justify a quoted figure of £1250 plus VAT by reference to either (a) the work that dealing with the application might require in a typical case, or (b) the work in fact done in the actual case, and in the circumstances the landlord's insistence on that figure was unreasonable.

The *Alienation Protocol* and the *Alterations Protocol* go into rather more detail, saying that the amount should take into account the complexity of the proposed transaction (including the number of leases, the volume of documents for review, the number of parties involved, and the number of documents to be drafted); the value of the property in question; any requirement to seek the consent of any other party (such as a lender or superior landlord); any need for external professional advice; any conditions requiring compliance; and any extraordinary feature of the proposed transaction.

Where the liability for costs exists, either through an undertaking or by virtue of the terms of the lease, and the amount of costs is disputed, it is open to a tenant to apply to have the landlord's solicitors' costs assessed by the court under *s.71, Solicitors Act 1974*. However, the case of *Tim Martin Interiors Ltd v Akin Gump LLP [2011] EWCA Civ 1574* illustrates that this may be of little help. The basis of assessment is the same as if it were the client itself applying to have the costs assessed under *s.70* of the 1974 Act. It is therefore presumed that costs were reasonably incurred, and reasonable in amount, so long as the solicitor had its client's approval to incur them.

It was suggested by the court in *Tim Martin Interiors* that the paying party who is really aggrieved may instead apply to court for an account of what sums are due, but few will take on the litigation risk involved in that.

Good and bad reasons

The *No 1 West India Quay* case raised another issue of general importance. The background was that a wealthy overseas investor had bought 42 apartments in an upmarket residential development in London's Docklands. They were all held on 999-year leases, under which landlord's consent was required to any assignment or sub-letting. The relationship between the investor and the landlord deteriorated, and the investor commenced a programme of disposals of all 42 flats.

Sales of the first eight proceeded smoothly enough, at prices between £500,000 and £1.165m, but in relation to sales of a further three flats the landlord sought to impose conditions on the grant of consent, including: (i) production of a bank reference in respect of the proposed assignee; (ii) an inspection of the flat by a surveyor, and payment of £350 plus VAT for the surveyor's fees; and (iii) payment of legal fees of £1250 plus VAT.

The investor tenant challenged the reasonableness of these conditions. As just stated, it was found that the landlord's insistence on an undertaking for legal costs of £1250 plus VAT was unreasonable. However, the court found that it *was* reasonable for the landlord to require a bank reference and to arrange for its surveyor to inspect the properties to check for breaches of covenant, despite the fact that these requirements were not specifically set out in the alienation covenant in the lease. Accordingly, the landlord was relying on both 'bad' and 'good' reasons.

The conventional understanding is that reliance on a bad reason does not vitiate any good reasons which are also relied upon, unless perhaps the bad reason is the real reason, and the others are just makeweights (*British Bakeries (Midlands) Ltd v Michael Testler & Co Ltd [1986] 1 EGLR 64*, and *BRS Northern Ltd v Templeheights Ltd [1998] 2 EGLR 182*). In *No 1 West India Quay*, though, the High Court held that since the landlord had insisted upon an undertaking for the figure of £1250 plus VAT as a pre-condition of considering the application for consent, that bad reason vitiated the good reasons, and prevented the landlord from relying upon them. The landlord was therefore held to have acted unreasonably.

This aspect of the decision was the subject of an appeal, reported at *No.1 West India Quay (Residential) Ltd v East Tower Apartments Ltd [2018] EWCA Civ 250*, and the Court of Appeal concluded that the landlord had *not* acted unreasonably. The theme running through the relevant caselaw was that if the decision would have been the same without reliance on the bad reason, then the decision (looked at overall) was good. In that situation the bad reason will not have vitiated or infected the good one.

The judge below had asked himself the wrong question. The question was not: would the landlord have maintained the unreasonable objection if the reasonable conditions had been complied with? Rather it was: would the landlord still have refused consent on the reasonable grounds, if it had not put forward the unreasonable ground? To put the point another way: the question is whether the decision to refuse consent was reasonable; not whether all the reasons for the decision were reasonable. Where, as here, the reasons were free-standing, each of them had causative effect, and two of them were reasonable, then the decision itself was reasonable.

As Lewison LJ commented:

> "*I consider that to hold otherwise might lead to considerable practical difficulties. The point can be tested this way. Imagine the case of a rack rented lease of valuable property where the rent is several*

hundred thousand pounds a year. The tenant asks for consent to assign. The landlord requires the tenant to pay his costs of, say, £1000 when a reasonable sum would be £750. However, the landlord also objects on well-reasoned and compelling grounds that the proposed assignee will be unable to pay the rent. It seems to me to be a draconian sanction if the landlord is to be saddled with a tenant of precarious financial means all for the sake of having demanded £250 too much as a fee."

Superior landlord's consent

If the lease under which consent is sought is a sub-lease, the fact that the superior landlord unreasonably refuses consent does not entitle the immediate landlord to refuse consent (*Vienit v Williams & Son (Bread Street) [1958] 1 WLR 1267*). The immediate landlord therefore finds itself in a difficult position: exposed to action by its tenant if it refuses consent, and exposed to the risk of forfeiture or other action by the superior landlord if it grants consent. Attempting to address the problem by granting consent conditional on the superior landlord's consent being granted may not succeed, since a conditional grant of consent may still be considered to be a grant of consent, and a breach of the terms of the head-lease. A preferable way forward is instead to require a covenant by the sub-tenant to obtain superior landlord's consent. If the sub-tenant fails to do so, then the sub-lease may be forfeited, protecting the immediate landlord's position as against the superior landlord.

Diminution in value of the reversion

Landlords are often inclined to object on the ground that the transaction proposed by the tenant will damage the value of their reversion. The court's approach to that in *International Drilling Fluids* has been seen: a perceived diminution in the value of the reversion is unlikely to be a proper and sufficient reason for withholding consent if the landlord has no intention of selling the reversion, or raising money upon it.

Further instances of that approach are *Ponderosa International Development v Pengap Securities [1986] 1 EGLR 66* and *FW Woolworth v Charlwood Alliance Properties [1987] 1 EGLR 53*).

Unlawful discrimination

Under *s.34, Equality Act 2010*, it is unlawful for a landlord to discriminate against a person by refusing to give permission for an assignment, sub-letting or parting with possession to them, on the basis of a protected characteristic within the meaning of the 2010 Act, namely: age, disability, gender reassignment, marriage and civil partnership, pregnancy and maternity, race, religion or belief, sex or sexual orientation. Under *s.35*, it is unlawful for a person who manages premises to discriminate against an occupier of the premises because of a protected characteristic by subjecting them to any detriment, and this may well be wide enough to apply to decisions in relation to any request for landlord's consent, not just alienation.

The fact that conduct is unlawful under the 2010 Act does not necessarily make it unreasonable at common law, but it seems highly unlikely that a court would consider a landlord's decision based on unlawful discrimination to be reasonable. Long before any anti-discrimination legislation, in *Mills v Cannon Brewery Co Ltd [1920] 2 Ch 38*, it was held that neither the name nor the nationality of a proposed assignee could amount to reasonable grounds for withholding consent.

Breaches of tenant's covenants

Landlords are sometimes inclined to regard an application for consent as leverage to have outstanding breaches of covenant rectified, or to 'tidy up' other outstanding management matters, such as an unresolved rent review. This does not sit well with the *International Drilling Fluids* guidelines: the landlord has its remedies in relation to breaches of covenant, and using the alienation, alterations or use covenants so as to give itself an additional remedy is a clear collateral advantage.

An outstanding breach of covenant will therefore not generally be regarded as a sufficient reason to refuse consent (*Beale v Worth [1993] EGCS 135*; *Farr v Ginnings [1928] 44 TLR 249*). A good modern example is provided by *Singh v Dhanji [2014] EWCA Civ 414*, which concerned an application for licence to assign a lease. The landlord discovered that the tenant had extensively refurbished the premises without his consent. The work, the costs of which amounted to some £140,000, involved moving two stud partition walls, replacing dental chairs and associated plumbing, replacing sinks, cupboards and other equipment, removing suspended ceilings and replacing flooring. The landlord served a number of notices under *s.146, Law of Property Act 1925* in relation to the work. He then wrote to the tenant informing her that his consent to the assignment was conditional upon the breaches specified in the s.146 notices being remedied.

Since the lease only prohibited structural alterations, and the county court found that the works carried out were non-structural, the only issue remaining for the Court of Appeal was whether the landlord had unreasonably withheld consent. The landlord need not have been right in believing there were breaches of covenant, so long as the belief was a reasonable one; to justify refusal, though, the breaches needed to have been sufficiently serious, and the Court held that they were minor in nature and of a kind which would not prejudice the landlord if not remedied until the end of the term. The landlord was held to have unreasonably withheld consent to the proposed assignment and an award of damages of £183,000, plus interest of £31,000 was upheld.

There is the odd example from caselaw in which the state of disrepair of the premises has been sufficiently serious to justify refusal (e.g. *Goldstein v Sanders [1915] 1 Ch 549*, where the condition of the property was described as "*little short of outrageous*"), but it is hard to draw any clear idea from the decided cases of how serious it needs to be.

If the landlord can show that a refusal of consent, or the imposition of a condition, is necessary to prevent his rights under the lease from being significantly prejudiced, then that may amount to a reasonable basis for refusing consent. An example might be where a tenant who is a good covenant, but who is in default of a repairing obligation, wants to assign to a much weaker covenant who is less likely to be able to meet the obligations at the end of the lease. *Orlando Investments Ltd v Grosvenor Estate (Belgravia) [1989] 43 EG 175* was an example where the breaches of covenant were substantial and long-standing, and the landlord had reasonable grounds to be concerned that the assignee would not address them. It was held to be reasonable to refuse consent. But if the assignee is just as good a covenant, or if the breach is not serious and can be just as easily dealt with by the assignee, the landlord is going to be in difficulties.

Risk of leasehold enfranchisement

There are a number of cases in which landlords have sought to refuse consent on the grounds that the tenant's proposed action, if permitted, would lead to leasehold enfranchisement, and the landlord being deprived of its property interest.

In *Norfolk Capital Group Ltd v Kitway [1977] 1 QB 506*, the landlord was held to have reasonably refused consent to an assignment. The proposed assignee was an individual, and if the assignment were to have proceeded, after five years' residence he would have been able to acquire the freehold under the *Leasehold Reform Act 1967*. This is four-square within the principles stated in *International Drilling Fluids*: the objection was based upon characteristics of the assignee, namely that he was an individual, who would therefore potentially acquire the entitlement to enfranchise.

In *Bickel v Duke of Westminster [1977] 1 QB 517*, the proposed transaction was again an assignment, this time to a sub-lessee in occupation. The tenant did not enjoy the right of enfranchisement under the *Leasehold Reform Act 1967* because they were not in occupation; the sub-lessee, because the rent payable under the sub-lease fell outside the qualifying limits. If the assignment proceeded, again the consequence would be that after five years' residence the assignee would be entitled to enfranchise.

Lord Denning MR considered the matter by reference to the 'dispro-portionate detriment' test, though not in so many words.

> "...it is a new situation, consequent on the Leasehold Reform Act 1967, which was never envisaged before. I would test it by considering first the position of the landlords, Grosvenor Estates. They hold a large estate which they desire to keep in their hands so as to develop it in the best possible way. This would be much impeded if one house after another was bought up by sitting tenants. Further, if they are compelled to sell under the 1967 Acts, they will suffer much financial loss, because the price is much less than the value of the house. Test it next by considering the position of the tenants, the Foresters. They hold the premises as an investment and want to sell it. It matters not to them whether they sell to the landlord or to sub-tenants, so long as they receive a fair price for it. The landlords say they are willing to negotiate a fair price for it. They will give the Foresters a sum equivalent to that offered by the sub-tenants. Test it next by considering the position of the sub-tenant herself. When she took her sub-lease, she had no possible claim to enfranchisement. It was at a high rent, outside the 1967 Act. She is quite well protected by the Rent Acts so far as her own occupation is concerned. She will not be evicted at the end of her term. The only result on her of a refusal will be that she will not be able to buy up the freehold for a very low figure."

The other members of the Court of Appeal preferred to dispose of the case on the basis of the first two principles stated in *International Drilling Fluids:* (a) the refusal was based upon the characteristics of the assignee; (b) enfranchisement clearly affected both the property which was the subject-matter of the lease, and the relationship between the landlord and the tenant.

The issue also arose in the context of alterations, and in relation to a commercial property, in *Mount Eden Land Ltd v Bolsover Investments Ltd [2014] EWHC 3523 (Ch)*. Mount Eden was the landlord of an office property in the West End of London; Bolsover was the tenant under a 999-year lease granted in 1926, and running from 1913. Bolsover applied for consent to carry out alterations to convert the property into 16 or 17 residential flats. The lease did not require landlord's consent to change the use, but did require landlord's consent to alterations. Mount Eden refused consent on the grounds that it was possible that the flats would be let on long leases, giving rise to a risk of collective leasehold enfranchisement.

Mount Eden naturally relied upon *Norfolk Capital Group Ltd v Kitway*, and *Bickel v Duke of Westminster*, arguing that a landlord was not acting unreasonably in seeking to preserve its property interests, and to avoid the possibility of compulsory enfranchisement.

The court distinguished the earlier cases. In those cases the landlord's concern was with the applicability of the *Leasehold Reform Act 1967*. Assignment of the lease from a company to an individual would give rise to a clear entitlement to enfranchise, and the statutory purchase price was only the site value. Here, the concern was with the scheme under the *Leasehold Reform (Housing and Urban Development) Act 1993*, in which the landlord would receive the open market value of its interest. Also, both cases concerned leases which were much shorter than the instant one, hence the landlord's interest was of much greater value.

The possibility of collective enfranchisement was speculative; Bolsover had not decided whether they would grant long- or short-term leases, and if they were to be short-term then collective enfranchisement would not be possible. Plus, the likelihood of the lessees acting collectively to enfranchise could not be known. It was so speculative as not to be a matter on which a reasonable landlord could rely.

Hautford Ltd v Rotrust Nominees Ltd [2018] EWCA Civ 765 has been discussed in chapter 3, in relation to the issue of collateral advantage. In this case the consent required was to the making of a change-of-use planning application in relation to a mixed-use property, the landlord refusing on the basis that the tenant's acknowledged aim to acquire the freehold by enfranchisement would be thereby made much more likely to succeed. The *Kitway* and *Bickel* cases were distinguished here because the lease had been granted after the enfranchisement legislation had been introduced; the landlord could have insisted upon restrictions specifically designed to make enfranchisement difficult or impossible, but could not rely upon the planning covenant in the lease to achieve the same objective, since that was outside the scope of what the planning covenants were there for.

It appears that whether a risk of leasehold enfranchisement will justify a landlord's refusal of consent depends very much on the specific context.

Summary

Certain questions have arisen for determination repeatedly, when reasonableness has been at issue:

- It is generally considered that a landlord can reasonably insist upon an undertaking to cover its reasonable costs being provided by the tenant, as a condition of granting consent. There is little that a tenant can easily do to challenge the amount of the costs.

- Where a landlord relies upon reasons which are 'bad', as well as some which are 'good', the general rule is that the bad reasons do not vitiate the good ones, and the decision may still be held to be reasonable.

- The fact that superior landlord's consent is also required, and is being unreasonably withheld, does not entitle the immediate landlord to refuse consent.

- An anticipated adverse impact of the tenant's proposed action on the value of the landlord's interest is unlikely to justify a landlord's refusal where the landlord has no intention of realising the value.

- A refusal based upon unlawful discrimination will almost certainly be unreasonable.

- A landlord who seeks to link consent to a condition that the tenant remedies some outstanding breach of covenant will probably be held to be unreasonable, though possibly not in cases of long-standing, serious breaches of covenant, where there is real doubt that a proposed assignee would or could remedy them.

- A risk of leasehold enfranchisement has been held to justify a landlord's refusal in certain cases, but not in others. It is a highly fact-sensitive issue.

CHAPTER FIVE
REASONABLENESS – ISSUES
SPECIFIC TO ASSIGNMENT

This chapter and the next address recurring issues in the assessment of reasonableness which are specific to the context of assignments and sub-lettings. In this one we cover assignments, while the next chapter deals with sub-lettings, but also some issues common to both types of transaction. The present chapter discusses the assessment of an assignee's covenant strength, requirements for the provision of security, the acceptability of overseas entities, and whether the benefit of a guarantor's covenant may be retained after the lease is assigned.

We have previously considered some recurring issues which may apply to any application for landlord's consent. This chapter now discusses issues which have relevance only in relation to requests for consent to an assignment of the lease.

Covenant strength of assignee

The first and most important of the *International Drilling Fluids* guidelines states that the purpose of the alienation restrictions in the lease is to protect the landlord from having his premises occupied by an undesirable tenant, or used in an undesirable way. It follows that the characteristics of the proposed assignee are a legitimate concern for the landlord in considering a request for licence to assign, and the most important characteristic will usually be whether the proposed assignee has adequate 'covenant strength': the financial means to pay the rent and to perform the other covenants in the lease, principally as to repair and payment of insurance premiums and service charge (if any). The landlord is entitled to be satisfied that the financial position of the assignee (taken together with the financial position of any guarantor) is sufficient for them to be able to pay the rent and comply with the lease covenants (*British Bakeries (Midlands) v Michael Testler & Co [1986] 1 EGLR 64*).

The judgment in that case provides a good example of the sort of examination of covenant strength which may be carried out. The tenant had provided six references, from: (1) the proposed assignees' accountants, (2) their bank, (3) their solicitor, (4) managing agents for their landlord of another property, and (5) and (6) two trade references. All were favourable, however they only referred to the referees' experience of the assignees' conduct of their existing business. In taking an assignment of the lease, they were proposing to embark upon a new business, additional to the existing one, so that most of the references were not fully on point. Moreover, the referees had all disclaimed liability, as is conventional. Some of them did state that the assignees should be good for the proposed new business, and the associated lease liabilities, but the judge was not satisfied that the referees had sufficient information to qualify them to give that view. As to the trade references, one gave no information as to the amount of business transacted with the assignees, and the other indicated that only some £300-£400 of business was done with them annually.

Three years' trading accounts had also been provided, but (a) they were unaudited, (b) the most recent was eighteen months old, and (c) they indicated only a modest amount of profits, so that the landlord had grounds for concern as to their ability to perform the lease covenants. Whether they were likely to be able to do so was dependent on the new venture generating sufficient profits.

In all the circumstances the landlord was not unreasonable in refusing consent.

It is often considered to be a 'rule of thumb' that an assignee should be able to show, over the last three years' accounts, average net profits equating to three times the passing rent: less than that, and the landlord can reasonably refuse consent to the assignment; more, and it cannot. This test was referred to in *British Bakeries (Midlands) v Michael Testler & Co*, and the accounts supplied for the proposed assignee failed it, though this was not a major factor in the decision.

In *Footwear Corporation v Amplight Properties [1999] 1 WLR 551*, the court stated that this is not a rule which the courts will recognise, and is not even to be regarded as a 'rule of thumb'. The assessment of covenant strength is more complex than simply applying an arithmetical formula, as *British Bakeries (Midlands) v Michael Testler & Co* demonstrates. In practice, it is still often the test which the landlord or its agent will apply, and accounts which fail this test are likely to prompt the landlord to seek legal advice on whether it can refuse consent.

British Bakeries (Midlands) v Michael Testler & Co shows that simply having references which are on their face favourable is far from being the end of the matter. Various references tend to feature in assessment of covenant strength, but their usefulness may be limited. Bank references mostly confine themselves to stating "X has been a client for Y years", which is hardly helpful, though it can at least be said that it would be worrying if a bank reference could not be supplied. Trade references will be coloured by the trading relationship between the parties: a supplier will not give a bad reference for one of their biggest customers. Landlords' references are perhaps the most likely to be of help.

It is conventional for the last three years' audited accounts to be supplied (filed accounts in the case of a company), and of course this is useful, indeed essential, information. That said, a set of accounts provides a snapshot as at the accounting date, and important context may be missing. Accounts may be prepared late, so the information may be months out of date. New start-ups will not have this accounting history, of course, so other information will be needed.

Any business plan which exists will probably be very helpful, since it enables the landlord to consider how the tenant's present financial position may develop, as a result of its plans – which of course may include, as in *British Bakeries (Midlands) v Michael Testler & Co*, starting a new business from the premises.

Credit references are likely to be obtained, and sometimes useful information is to be found in local press coverage, or even social media.

It is comparatively uncommon for landlords simply to issue a refusal, when covenant strength is the issue. It is more likely that the landlord will be prepared to consent, but only on condition that adequate security is supplied. This may take the form of a guarantee from a parent company, one or more individual directors, or a bank; or it may take the form of a rent deposit. Other forms of security, such as a bank bond, are less common. The issue is then whether it is reasonable for the landlord to require that security, which entails a view on (a) the reasonableness of the landlord's concern as to covenant strength, as well as (b) the reasonableness of the requirement for the specific security.

If the tenant offers the provision of a guarantor, the landlord then needs to investigate the financial strength of the proposed guarantor as well. In *Mount Eden Land v Towerstone [2002] 31 EG 97 (CS)*, a landlord was reasonable in refusing consent to an assignment where guarantors had been required, and the guarantors' references did not speak as to their ability to meet all their contingent liabilities, rather than just their ability to meet the financial obligations arising under the lease. The guarantors had given guarantees already in relation to a number of other leases held by the proposed assignee company, so that if the company failed, the demands on them would have been much more than just meeting the obligations under the one lease.

When it is the financial strength of an individual which is to be assessed, there are of course no filed accounts as such. As well as refer-ences, the landlord will certainly wish to see trading accounts, but may also require a range of information which may appear intrusive: bank statements, mortgage statements, tax returns and VAT returns.

Alienation Protocol

The *Alienation Protocol* reflects the need to carry out this financial assessment, providing that when an application for landlord's consent to a dealing with the property is made:

- It should specify the nature of the transaction and identify the assignee/sub-tenant, together with any guarantor.

- It should include sufficient information about the assignee/sub-tenant (and any guarantor), including:

  ○ A description of their trade or business

  ○ Registered number and office, in the case of companies

  ○ In the case of individuals, references or referees' contact details

- In the case of an application for consent to assign, the information on the assignee should include information demonstrating that the assignee (and any guarantor) will be able to comply with the lease obligations. This may, it is stated, include the last three years' accounts, or a business plan with profit forecasts.

As the *Alienation Protocol* acknowledges, this guidance is a good starting-point, but can never be a complete list for every situation, since circumstances will differ.

Covenant strength of assignor

In relation to leases granted pre-1996, prior to the coming into force of the *Landlord and Tenant (Covenants) Act 1995*, the assigning tenant will remain liable for the performance of the tenant's covenants after the assignment. In the case of post-1995 leases, the landlord will often be able to require the assigning tenant to guarantee the obligations of its immediate assignee by means of an Authorised Guarantee Agreement, or 'AGA'. In either situation, where the assigning tenant is a very strong covenant, there may be a question how far the landlord is entitled to be concerned about the covenant strength of the proposed assignee.

In *Royal Bank of Scotland v Victoria Street (No. 3) Limited [2008] EWHC 3052 (Ch)*, the High Court confirmed that a landlord does not have to take into account whether being able to continue to enforce the covenants against the assigning tenant would give enough security against default by the assignee.

"In my judgment, a landlord can object to the covenant strength of the assignee where the landlord is concerned in a practical way about the payment of rent and the performance and observance of the covenants, even where the landlord has the benefit of the original tenant's covenant."

Retaining benefit of existing guarantee

Where a guarantee has been given in relation to tenant's obligations under a lease, the landlord may wish, upon any assignment, to retain the benefit of that guarantee. The lease may have been granted to a start-up, or a non-trading company within a group, or simply to a company of inadequate financial strength, and the lease perhaps would not have been granted at all, had it not been for the availability of an acceptable guarantor. It is no use to the landlord to be able to rely upon the covenant of the assignor, once the assignment has taken place; it needs to be able to rely upon that of the guarantor.

In the case of a pre-1996 lease, to which the *Landlord and Tenant (Covenants) Act 1995* does not apply, the landlord will retain the benefit of the covenants of both the assignor and its guarantor, by operation of privity of contract. It is in the case of post-1995 leases that there is a problem.

One of the most important question marks hanging over the operation of the 1995 Act has always been whether a tenant's guarantor can be required to guarantee the obligations of the assignee. As the tenant is automatically released upon the assignment pursuant to *s.5*, so *s.24(2)* provides for the automatic release of the guarantor at the same time. If the landlord requires, as a condition of granting consent to an assignment, that the assignor's guarantor now enter into a fresh guarantee of the assignee's obligations, the question arises whether this arrangement falls foul of the anti-avoidance provision contained in *s.25(1)*:

"any agreement relating to a tenancy is void to the extent that it would apart from this section have effect to exclude, modify or otherwise frustrate the operation of any provision of this Act."

This issue has been the subject of much debate, and the uncertainty has in some respects been dispelled by a quintet of important cases, from 2010 to 2016:

- *Good Harvest Partnership LLP v Centaur Services Ltd [2010] EWHC 330 (Ch)*

- *K/S Victoria Street v House of Fraser (Stores Management) Ltd and others [2011] EWCA Civ 904*

- *Tindall Cobham 1 Limited v Adda Hotels [2014] EWHC 2637 (Ch)*

- *Zinc Cobham 1 Limited v Adda Hotels [2015] EWHC 53 (Ch)*

- *EMI Group Ltd v O & H Q1 Ltd [2016] EWHC 529 (Ch)*

However, those cases have raised just as many new uncertainties, at least partly because much of what the judges have said in them is *obiter*. What can be said with certainty is that the so-called 'repeat guarantee' structure, requiring the assignor's guarantor to guarantee the obligations of the assignee under the lease, falls foul of *s.25(1)* and is void.

The lease may expressly require a repeat guarantee, and *Tindall Cobham 1 Limited v Adda Hotels* shows that the court, faced with that situation, will effectively rewrite the lease to omit that void requirement, while striving to find a way of keeping the alienation provisions workable. In the absence of any such requirement in the lease it is unlikely that a landlord would require a repeat guarantee, in the light of the caselaw. Should it do so, the clear authority that the arrangement would be void must make the requirement unreasonable.

An alternative structure, however, is thought to work: the so-called 'sub-AGA', or 'GAGA' (Guarantee of an Authorised Guarantee Agreement). This works by requiring the assignor's guarantor to guarantee, not the assignee's obligations under the lease, but the obligations of the assignor under an AGA. In pounds and pence the outcome is exactly the same as the repeat guarantee structure; it is simply arrived at by going around the other two sides of the rectangle. Strictly speaking, judicial pronouncements approving the GAGA structure have all been *obiter* to date, but it is widely considered to work.

On an assignment, a landlord may well require that the assignor's guarantor enter into a GAGA. Probably the ability to require this will be drafted for, either as a condition precedent, or as a s.19(1A) provision, in which case the landlord can insist on it, reasonable or otherwise. If not, the assessment of whether it is reasonable to require it is no different from the assessment of the landlord's reasonableness in requiring the provision of any other form of security.

Other possible structures can be devised. A landlord could conceivably attempt to retain the benefit of the guarantee by requiring that the lease be first assigned to the guarantor, so that an AGA could be required from it upon a further assignment; or perhaps that the lease be assigned to the proposed assignee *together* with the guarantor, as joint tenants. The problem with either course is that there is authority to the effect that an assignment to the assignor's guarantor would also be void. This was stated *obiter* in *K/S Victoria Street*, and formed part of the ratio in *EMI Group Ltd*. It is therefore highly likely that such a requirement would be unreasonable.

It is worth reminding ourselves that these issues do not apply to pre-1996 leases - although of course they are now the minority.

Overseas entities

Where a proposed assignee is an overseas company, or an individual resident abroad, the landlord may have concerns about the ability in practical terms to enforce the lease covenants against them, since this may require serving proceedings or other documents overseas, registering any domestic judgment in a foreign court, and perhaps selling foreign assets in satisfaction of the judgment. This issue frequently arises where the proposed assignee is a subsidiary of an overseas corporation, and offers that corporation as guarantor.

The fact that a proposed assignee or guarantor is a foreign entity is not in itself a reasonable ground for refusing consent. Like most matters when assessing reasonableness, it will depend on the specific facts. In *Kened v Connie Investments [1997] 1 EGLR 21*, a company called Kuwaiti Algerian Investment Company SA was offered as a guarantor. It was incorporated in Luxembourg, carried on activities mostly in Algeria, and while it had substantial assets, they were outside the jurisdiction.

It was held to be unreasonable for the landlord to refuse to accept them as guarantor.

- Luxembourg is a signatory of the Brussels Convention, and enforcing an English judgment would there present only a minor additional inconvenience, which a reasonable landlord would not regard as a sufficient reason to withhold consent. An irrevocable nomination of an address for service within the jurisdiction would be provided.

- The proposed guarantor was a substantial company owned equally by the Kuwaiti and Algerian Governments, both heavily engaged in international trade and unlikely to wish to allow their subsidiaries to default on their commercial undertakings. To overcome the objection based on the absence of assets within the jurisdiction, it had moreover offered a rent deposit in an amount equating to one year's rent (£375,000).

A different conclusion might of course be reached in the case of a non-Brussels Convention country, where the concern over a lack of assets within the jurisdiction could not be addressed by the matters relied on by the judge in this case.

Over-rented properties and incentives

When a tenant comes to market its lease, there will be an obvious problem if the rental market has fallen, so that the rent being paid is higher than the market level; the premises are then said to be 'over-rented'. The only way in which anyone will be persuaded to take an assignment of the lease in these circumstances is if the assigning tenant provides them with an incentive of some sort to induce them to take the assignment. This may be in the shape of payment of a capital sum (a 'reverse premium'), or perhaps a rent subsidy.

It is unusual for the alienation clause in the lease to prohibit this, although the landlord may not be happy about it, since it will be adverse market evidence which may be used against it on rent reviews or lease renewals of other properties. The tenant may therefore prefer not to disclose the arrangement to the landlord, and there is no obligation to do so. This was one of the issues in *Kened v Connie Investments Ltd [1997] 1 EGLR 21*, where the judge held:

> "*Of course the landlord is entitled to be informed of anything which bears upon the giving of his consent. If there was anything in the assignment which would affect him, then the tenant was obliged to provide that information to him. But I can see no reason why the landlord would be interested in the details of the assignment... The relationship between the landlord and the assignee will be governed by the terms of the [lease] and not by the terms of the assignment. In an ordinary case where the assignment is made at a premium the landlord is not normally told, and does not normally inquire, as to the amount of the premium, even though the payment of the premium by the assignee will to that extent diminish the assignee's*

financial resources and hence his ability to comply with the covenants in the lease."

In the case of an application for licence to assign, the landlord is concerned only with the identity and character of the assignee, and not with the terms of the transaction.

An incentive arrangement may perhaps suggest that the assignee is not, without the benefit of that incentive, of adequate financial strength. However, this would form only a part of the whole picture when assessing the covenant strength.

Summary

The covenant strength of a proposed assignee, and/or its guarantor, is very much a ground on which a landlord can reasonably rely, when refusing consent or imposing conditions, provided the factual assessment of the financial position is reasonable.

The assessment of a party's financial condition can be a complex and wide-ranging enquiry in some cases. A landlord who has a concern about covenant strength may well require some security to be provided, rather than refusing consent outright, and in that case the reasonableness of the requirement for the specific form of security will also be a potential issue.

As regards parties with existing liability on the lease covenants:

- the strength of an existing tenant who will remain liable after the assignment does not prevent a landlord from objecting to the financial weakness of the proposed assignee; and

- in relation to post-1995 leases, it is likely that the only way in which the benefit of an existing guarantor's covenant can be retained is by requiring them to guarantee the obligations which the assignor will be assuming under an Authorised Guarantee Agreement.

Landlords often have concerns about overseas assignees or guarantors, and whether it is reasonable to object to them is fact-dependent.

When a property is over-rented, and it can only be assigned by offering a rent subsidy or some other incentive to the incoming party, this is something which the landlord may not take into account in its decision.

CHAPTER SIX

REASONABLENESS – ISSUES SPECIFIC TO SUB-LETTING; ISSUES COMMON TO BOTH ASSIGNMENT AND SUB-LETTING

This chapter addresses recurring issues in the assessment of reasonableness which are specific to the context of sub-lettings. It goes on to consider certain issues common to both assignment and sub-letting. The issue of covenant strength in relation to sub-tenants is discussed first, and then the means by which tenants may overcome restrictions upon the rental level which must be achieved upon any sub-letting. Issues common to both assignment and sub-letting are (a) objections based upon the proposed use of the premises, particularly issues relating to retail properties and tenant mix policies, and (b) the reasonableness of requiring direct covenants from assignees, sub-tenants and guarantors.

We have previously considered some recurring issues which may apply to any application for landlord's consent, and also considerations which are specific to consent to assignments. We now go on to look at issues which have relevance only to sub-lettings.

Covenant strength

If a landlord has reasonable concerns about the covenant strength of a prospective assignee, and no acceptable security can be provided, the tenant may seek to sub-let the premises instead. This is a second-best option from the tenant's point of view, since it retains liability on the lease covenants as tenant. For the same reason, though, the covenant strength of the prospective sub-tenant is not so important as that of a prospective assignee, and therefore it is much harder for a landlord to resist on that ground (e.g. *Mount Eden Land v Folia [2003] EWHC 1815 (Ch)*).

As always, this observation must yield to circumstances. Suppose a lease which does not require that sub-leases be contracted-out of the *Landlord and Tenant Act 1954*, and a tenant who applies for landlord's consent to sub-let, near the end of the term. The result of the sub-letting, if it were to proceed, would be that the sub-tenant would shortly find itself in a position to renew its lease directly against the landlord, and the current tenant would drop out of the picture. In those circumstances, it is suggested that the landlord would very properly and reasonably be interested in the covenant strength of the proposed sub-tenant.

Rent restrictions

As in the case of an assignment, if the premises are over-rented, the only way of marketing them is likely to be by offering an incentive to the sub-tenant. Unlike in the case of an assignment, the arrangement must be disclosed to the landlord. As long ago as *Fuller's Theatre & Vaudeville Co v Rofe [1923] AC 435*, it was established that in the case of a proposed underletting, the landlord is entitled to know the terms on which the underletting is to take place. The terms on which the property is occupied by the sub-tenant may come to bind the landlord in the event of surrender, renewal, disclaimer or forfeiture of the head-lease. For that reason, as well as the impact on rental evidence for rent reviews or lease renewals on other properties, the landlord will be concerned about any rent subsidy.

It is not unknown for tenants to try to persuade their advisers that any such incentive should not be disclosed to the landlord, but of course this must be resisted. If the landlord's consent were to be procured by deception, the tenant having withheld information about a rent subsidy arrangement, the consent would be liable to be set aside. The professional advisers would be in difficulty as regards their professional conduct obligations, if they were to be party to a deception.

It is highly likely that the lease will contain provision concerning the rental level of any sub-letting. Most commercial leases will provide that the premises are not to be sub-let at less than the market rent, or sometimes the passing rent, and without taking a fine or premium. A distinction needs to be made between the 'market rent' type of restriction, and the 'passing rent' type of restriction, although landlords tend to conflate the two; if the tenant proposes to sub-let at something less than the passing rent, the landlord is apt to consider that the proposed rental is at less than the market level. Tenants anticipate that their landlord will react in this way, and therefore also tend to treat the two types of restriction alike.

In either case, the rental restriction will almost certainly be a condition precedent to the ability to sub-let, so that unless and until it is shown that it has been satisfied, no reasonableness requirement applies. As it happens, although strictly *obiter*, the judge concluded in *Allied Dunbar Assurance v Homebase [2002] 1 P&CR 1* that an objection to the rental level which was motivated by a wish to prevent adverse rental evidence being generated was unreasonable.

'Market rent' restriction

An obvious way to address a disagreement over what is the market rent, in evidential terms, is by competing expert valuation evidence, which can make for uncertain and risky litigation. However, tenants were given a considerable helping hand by the case of *Blockbuster Entertainment v Leakcliff Properties [1997] 1 EGLR 28*, where it was held that if the tenant has marketed the premises properly, and accepted the best rental offer which it has been able to obtain, that will usually be the best evidence of what is market value.

> "*I have reached the clear conclusion that the tenant's best evidence of what a particular property is worth on the open market is the rent payable under a binding agreement for the letting of the property after it has been properly exposed to the market. Of course, if it can be shown that the property has been marketed incompetently or that, for some special reason of the intending lessor, the property has not been properly exposed to the market, one may well conclude that the highest firm bid received as a result of the marketing exercise does not*

in fact represent the market value of the property concerned… having decided that the marketing campaign was an effective one that produced the open market rent, it seems to me that the weight to be given to the expert evidence is comparatively slight on this issue."

This approach was confirmed in *Allied Dunbar Assurance v Homebase*.

A landlord who wants to attack a proposed sub-letting on the basis that the rent is below the market level will therefore need not only very cogent expert evidence on value, but also evidence of serious flaws in the marketing of the property.

'Passing rent' restriction

It is a much easier matter for the landlord to show breach of a passing rent restriction; this is simple arithmetic. A possible approach for the tenant trying to circumvent the issue is to enter into a side deed, or collateral agreement, with the sub-tenant, so that while the apparent rent is the same as the passing rent, the actual rent will be lower. As stated above, the proposed side deed must be disclosed to the landlord.

Allied Dunbar Assurance v Homebase was an instance of the tenant treating a market rent restriction as if it were a passing rent restriction. The lease contained pre-conditions to the ability to sub-let: any sub-letting should be at no less than the market rent, and also on all the same terms as the head-lease. In the market conditions at the time, the rent achievable on all the head-lease terms would have been significantly below the passing rent. The tenant might have simply marketed the premises on those terms, and defended the deal eventually done as the best evidence of market value, but it did not adopt that approach.

Presumably anticipating that the rent achievable on that basis would be challenged by the landlord, it attempted to forestall any objection by proposing to grant a sub-lease at the same rent as that passing under the head-lease, and on all the terms of the head-lease. Concessions had to be given to the sub-tenant to induce them to enter into a sub-lease on those terms, and they were to be contained in a collateral agreement with the sub-tenant, personal to the parties. The concessions had the effect of applying a reduced rent on a stepped basis over a seven-year period (and thereby effectively fixing the next two rent reviews), and restricting the sub-tenant's repairing liability.

The side deed was quite properly disclosed to the landlord. The tenant's position was that the landlord could not object to the transaction on the basis of the contents of the deed. It was a personal arrangement, and the proposed sub-lease for which landlord's consent was sought was fully compliant with the conditions set out in the head-lease.

The court held that the two documents must be read together. It was unrealistic to suggest that the terms of the deal between the tenant and the sub-tenant could be found by looking only at the proposed sub-lease, without reference to the side deed. The terms were contained in the two documents. It did not matter that the collateral agreement was expressed to be personal as between the parties to it, because there would be a risk that on renewal the sub-lease terms as varied by the collateral agreement would be carried over into a new tenancy.

Therefore the head-lease conditions were not satisfied, the tenant was not entitled to sub-let on that basis, and no reasonableness requirement applied.

Although the case was concerned with a market rent restriction, the decision in *Allied Dunbar Assurance v Homebase* potentially presented a serious problem for tenants subject to passing rent restrictions. The side deed solution had been, until then, in common use in relation to passing rent restrictions, where the favourable caselaw in relation to ascertaining the market rent, mentioned above, could not assist.

A solution was offered by *NCR Ltd v Riverland Portfolio No 1 Ltd (No. 1) [2004] 16 EG 110 (CS)*. In that case, the lease contained a passing rent restriction. The tenant proposed to sub-let at the passing rent, in compliance with the lease, but at the same time proposed to pay the sub-tenant a reverse premium to induce it to do so. The court held that that did not amount to a variation of the terms of the sub-lease, and so did not fall foul of *Allied Dunbar Assurance v Homebase*. If the landlord needed at some point in the future to enforce the terms of the sub-lease against the sub-tenant – after a surrender of the head-lease, say – those terms would be enforceable in full. The rent as stated in the sub-lease would genuinely be the rent payable under the sub-lease. It was immaterial that the amount of the premium might have been calculated to be the equivalent of a rent subsidy.

One possible objection to this solution is that leases commonly provide that any sub-letting shall not be *"at a fine or premium"*. The purpose of this is commonly held to be to prevent the tenant from stripping out the capital value of the lease by *receiving* a premium; it is not to prevent the tenant from paying a reverse premium. Unless there is some specific prohibition on paying a reverse premium, therefore, this should not be an obstacle.

While this reverse premium solution works, the limitation in practical terms is that the tenant may not have the resources to pay a substantial sum to a sub-tenant. Another solution has been suggested by a number of respected commentators. The rationale of *Allied Dunbar Assurance v Homebase* is that where A and B have entered into a sub-lease on certain terms, and also a further document which varies those terms and provides for A to refund B a portion of the rent, it is not open to them to characterise the arrangement between them as being represented simply by the unvaried sub-lease. The same consideration does not apply if A and B enter into the sub-lease, but it is A's group company C which enters into the side deed and makes the refund. The arrangement between A and B can quite accurately be characterised as being that set out in the sub-lease. This is logical, but has not yet been tested in a decided case.

In any event, these issues do not have the practical importance which they had in the difficult economic circumstances of the early 1990s and 2000s. In April 2005, 41 major commercial landlords issued a Declaration on Sub-letting, stating that in new leases they would in future only require market rent restrictions not passing rent restrictions, and that where existing leases contained passing rent restrictions, they would not enforce them. The *Code for Leasing Business Premises in England and Wales* also recommends that leases should not contain passing rent restrictions. As a result, they are much less commonly encountered, and indeed may be unattractive to landlords because they can be perceived to be onerous, and therefore potentially result in lower rents being determined upon any rent review.

Alienation Protocol

These issues specific to sub-lettings are reflected in the terms of the *Alienation Protocol*, which provides that when an application for landlord's consent to a sub-letting of the property is made, it should be accompanied by a draft sub-lease, or at least detailed heads of terms. There is no provision in relation to supplying financial information on the proposed sub-tenant.

Issues common to both assignment and sub-letting

We have discussed, in this chapter and the previous one, recurring issues as to reasonableness as regards assignment, and as regards sub-lettings. Some issues apply to both types of transaction, though.

Use

It may be recalled that in accordance with the *International Drilling Fluids* principles it may be reasonable for the landlord to object to an assignment/sub-letting on the basis of the intended use of the premises, even though that use may not be prohibited by the lease. The *Alienation Protocol* requires the tenant to include with its application, whether relating to assignment or sub-letting, information as to the proposed use of the premises.

There are two questions which tend to arise together, where use is concerned. First, would the prospective use be in breach of the user covenant? Secondly, would that use give rise to an adverse impact on other tenants, or be objectionable in other ways?

Prospective breach of user covenant

There may be a preliminary consideration here, where the lease contains a fully qualified prohibition, i.e. change of use is prohibited, unless with landlord's consent, not to be unreasonably withheld. In those circumstances, the new use could only be a breach of covenant if it would be reasonable for the landlord to refuse consent to it. It follows that the objectionableness of the use would have to be determined in order to deal with the issue of prospective breach, so that the two issues may become conflated.

If, however, there is no reasonableness restriction as regards change of use, or no provision for change of use at all, it might seem a straightforward matter. If the assignment or sub-letting would involve a breach of user covenant, surely it must be reasonable for the landlord to refuse?

Surprisingly, there was for some years binding authority to the opposite effect, in *Killick v Second Covent Garden Property Co [1973] 1 WLR 658*. The case has been judicially described as "*startling*", and stigmatised as the "*refuge of the desperate*". In that case it was held that it could not be reasonable for a landlord to object to an assignment on the ground that the assignee's intended use of the premises would be in breach of covenant, since the landlord would always be able to enforce the user covenant against the assignee. While that was an accurate analysis of the landlord's rights, it was hardly a helpful or practical decision. The rigidity of that conclusion gave it the character of a proposition of law, rather than a judgment of fact in a specific context.

The decision was disapproved in *Ashworth Frazer v Gloucester City Council [2001] 3 WLR 2180*. The House of Lords in that case considered that the landlord could quite reasonably take into account the prospect of having to become involved in expensive and uncertain litigation with the assignee over the use of the property. The position following *Ashworth Frazer* is that it may be reasonable for a landlord to refuse consent on the grounds of prospective breach of user covenant. Their Lordships emphasised the conventional position that what is or is not reasonable is to be decided as a question of fact in all the circumstances of the specific case; hence, while it is probable that a prospective breach of user covenant would be a reasonable ground for refusing consent, there may be circumstances in which it would not. The *Killick* rule, that it can *never* be reasonable, has not been replaced with an equally rigid rule that it will *always* be reasonable.

Impact on other tenants

Disputes over change of use arise most commonly in the retail context, where the landlord often owns a wider development in which the subject premises are situated. This may be a small parade of shops, where the landlord wishes to preserve a range of different trades, both to make it attractive to local shoppers, and also to protect the tenants from competition. It may, alternatively, be a large shopping centre, where having the right mix of tenants, situated in the right places in the centre, encourages shoppers to remain in the centre for longer and to buy more.

The latter type of situation arose in *Moss Bros Group v CSC Properties [1999] EGCS 47*, where the landlord's policy was to concentrate retail fashion uses in a particular part of the shopping centre. The tenant, whose unit was situated in that part of the centre, requested consent to assign to a computer games retailer. It was held to be reasonable for the landlord to refuse consent. There was in fact no written policy, though the landlord could demonstrate a consistent policy in its decision-making. Clearly it would have been easier for the landlord if there had been a written tenant mix policy, which had been communicated to the tenants, and major retail landlords now generally make sure that this is done in relation to each of their developments. This was one case in which the court considered carefully whether the detriment to the tenant of the refusal of consent outweighed the benefit to the landlord of maintaining its tenant mix policy, and concluded that it did not. The court recognised, however, that there might be cases where the opposite conclusion could be reached.

While a landlord might want to concentrate a particular type of retail use in a particular part of its development, there may come a point where saturation point is reached, and the presence of another competitor could be expected to have adverse consequences. There is a Canadian case, *Coopers & Lybrand v William Schwartz Construction Co (1980) 116 DLR (3d) 450*, where the landlord was held to be reasonable in refusing consent where the intended assignee's user would increase competition to an excessive degree within the shopping centre, so that the viability of other tenants' businesses might be threatened.

That concern is more likely to arise in relation to small parades of shops. In a lease renewal case in the Central London County Court, *Martin Retail Group Ltd v Crawley Borough Council [2013] EW Misc 32 CC*, a local authority landlord, of just that sort of retail development, sought to protect demarcation between the different retail uses in the parade by introducing into the renewal lease a prohibition on selling certain products. The proposed clause was held to be anti-competitive, under the *Competition Act 1998*. The decision came as a surprise, since most commentary on the 1998 Act in its application to land agreements, including the guidance issued by the Competition and Markets Authority, indicated that use clauses in leases were unlikely to fall foul of it.

The manner in which the landlord conducted that case is in some ways puzzling, and it is perhaps a one-off, but it suggests some wider implications. The landlord there had not given exclusivity covenants to the other retailers, but one can imagine a situation in which a landlord refuses consent to an assignment to, say, a butcher, on the grounds that consenting would place the landlord in breach of an exclusivity covenant with a butcher already trading in the development. The assigning tenant might then challenge that covenant as anti-competitive, and that is very much the type of provision which is considered to be the target of the *Competition Act 1998*.

Landlord resisting assignments on the grounds of excessive competition will have to give careful consideration to *Competition Act* considerations.

Direct covenants

In relation to pre-1996 leases, to which the *Landlord and Tenant (Covenants) Act 1995* does not apply, a landlord will invariably require that the assignee gives in the licence to assign a covenant directly with the landlord to pay the rent and perform the tenant's covenants in the lease, not just for the period that the assignee is the tenant, but for the whole of the remainder of the term. There is no authority on whether this is reasonable. It is at least arguable, in the light of the policy of the 1995 Act, that it is not.

In the same way, upon consenting to a sub-letting the landlord is likely to require from the sub-tenant a direct covenant to observe all the tenant's covenants contained in the head-lease. In *Balfour v Kensington Gardens Mansions Ltd [1932] 49 TLR 49*, that was held to be unreasonable, though the short report does not discuss the reasons. It does appear, though, that the sub-lease was to be granted at an annual rent of £450, while the head-lease reserved a rent of £700 per annum, so perhaps little explanation is needed. It is usual for a sub-tenant to give such a direct covenant if required, though, as suggested by the case, a significant disparity between the content of the covenants in the proposed sub-lease and those in the head-lease might make the requirement unreasonable. For example, the head-lease might contain a full repairing covenant, while that in the proposed sub-lease might be limited by reference to a schedule of condition.

In relation to a requirement for a guarantor, it has been held that it was not reasonable to require the guarantor to assume liability throughout the term (*Evans v Levy [1910] 1 Ch 452*). It may be more reasonable for the guarantor's liability to be co-terminous with that of the party whose obligations are guaranteed. The usual note of caution applies: *Evans v Levy* was a decision on the facts of a specific case, not a principle of general application. This is not an issue in relation to post-1995 leases, since in those cases the *Landlord and Tenant (Covenants) Act 1995* provides that the guarantor of an assignee is released automatically upon any further assignment.

Summary

The covenant strength of a proposed sub-tenant is generally not a matter with which a landlord is entitled to be concerned.

Leases often contain a restriction on the level of rent which must be achieved upon a sub-letting, and this can be problematic where premises are over-rented, and can only be sub-let by offering some incentive to a sub-tenant, such as a rent subsidy. Any such arrangement must be disclosed to the landlord. There ways around the problem:

- If the restriction provides that the best market rent must be achieved, a tenant who has marketed the property competently has the best evidence of market rental, in the form of the deal which it has done.

- If the restriction provides that the rent on any sub-letting must be no less that the rent passing under the head-lease, the tenant can achieve this by paying a sub-tenant a reverse premium to induce them to enter into the sub-lease, and the landlord may not object on that basis.

It may be reasonable for a landlord to object to an assignment or sub-letting on the grounds that the intended use of the property will be in breach of covenant. Even if it will not be in breach of covenant, a landlord may still be reasonable in objecting to it, and a common reason in the retail context is the landlord's policy as to the combination of retail uses desired in its development. Landlords who object to an intended use because they wish to protect existing tenants from competition must think about any implication from competition law.

Where a landlord seeks to impose as a condition of consent that direct covenants to observe the covenants in the lease are given by assignees, guarantors or sub-tenants, there is potential to argue whether these are reasonable in duration or in principle, though there is relatively little authority and this must be fact-dependent.

CHAPTER SEVEN
CONSENTS WHICH AMOUNT
TO LEASE VARIATION

This chapter deals with situations in which what appears to be a landlord's consent actually effects a variation of the lease. This may be where the tenant seeks consent to carry out works which fall outside the demise, or it may be where the action for which consent is sought is absolutely prohibited by the lease. The risks discussed are implied surrender and regrant of the lease by operation of law, and releasing or limiting the right of recourse against guarantors or former tenants.

The issue

The fact that a particular action may be absolutely prohibited by the terms of the lease does not mean that it cannot be undertaken. The landlord may be persuaded that it is a good idea, or at least not a bad one, and be prepared to permit it. If so, the permission, properly analysed, will amount to something more than just a consent.

A good example of this was provided by the case of *Topland Portfolio No 1 Ltd v Smiths News Trading Ltd [2014] EWCA Civ 18*. In that case, Do-it-All was the tenant of a retail DIY warehouse, and requested landlord's consent to carry out various works. The lease contained an absolute prohibition on all but internal works, and defined the demised premises to include any alterations and additions. The works proposed by the tenant went well beyond internal works, consisting principally of knocking through an external wall in order to construct an entirely new garden centre outside the building. The landlord was happy with the proposals nevertheless, and consent was documented by a licence to alter.

The court held that the licence to alter had actually effected a variation of the lease. The works could not be carried out without a clear breach of covenant, if not for the licence. A change to the tenant's obligations must therefore have been effected; it was more than a concession, and it did not matter that it was a one-off, and that apart from those specific works the absolute prohibition on alterations continued. The fact that the demised premises were defined to include alterations and additions did not mean that the lease had sufficient flexibility that works of this nature and magnitude could be carried out with requiring a variation.

(The latter point indicates that, as one would expect, the question must turn on construction of the lease in any specific instance. Potentially, other terms of the lease might point to the conclusion that no variation of the lease was implied by the consent.)

The consequences of the lease having been varied can be significant, as they were in *Topland*, and we shall return to them shortly.

As well as consent to carry out works which are absolutely prohibited, another surprisingly common situation in relation to alterations, which raises the same issue, is a tenant asking for consent to carry out works outside the premises. For example, the tenant of one floor of an office building may ask for consent to place some equipment on the roof, and install cabling between the equipment and its floor. Another common situation is the tenant proposing to install some air-conditioning plant at the exterior of the premises, and this may well extend beyond the demise.

That is almost certainly not going to be envisaged by the lease. The lease will set out what works the tenant is entitled to do within the demised premises, but it is not likely to contemplate permitting the tenant to carry out works outside the premises. Where the landlord consents to works which entail putting equipment onto a part of the landlord's property that is not within the tenant's demise, the landlord may in reality be extending the demise, or at the least granting some form of additional licence to occupy. The licence to alter will therefore effectively constitute a deed of variation to the lease, as well as a licence to carry out works.

It is for this reason that the *Alterations Protocol* provides that when an application is made for consent to alterations, it should identify:

- whether the proposed alterations fall within the demised premises;

- whether the proposed alterations are structural or non-structural;

- the works for which the landlord's consent is needed;

- any works for which the landlord's consent is not needed;

- those works which are (i) absolutely prohibited under the terms of the lease so that the landlord has an unfettered right to withhold consent and (ii) those works from which the landlord may withhold consent only where it is reasonable.

It would be very helpful if applications for consent followed this recommendation, although few do.

While the issue is one which commonly arises in the context of alterations, it has relevance in other consent contexts, too. For example, a landlord might be agreeable to a change of use, or a sharing of occupation, despite there being an absolute prohibition in the lease.

The licence/variation confusion can have important consequences.

Implied surrender and regrant

One of the possible consequences of an unintended lease variation is the lease being impliedly surrendered by operation of law, to be replaced by a new lease on the varied terms.

A surrender of a lease by operation of law occurs on any occasion where the actions of the parties demonstrate that they intend to bring a lease to an end. One such occasion is when a new lease is granted to a person in respect of premises of which that person is already the tenant. The law cannot accommodate two leases of the same premises, covering the same period of time, between the same people. The legal consequence is therefore that the first lease is effectively surrendered by operation of law, and a new lease on the varied terms has been granted in its place.

The circumstances in which this might happen as a consequence of a lease variation were fully considered in *Friends Provident Life Office v British Railways Board [1995] 2 EGLR 55*. In that case, British Railways Board had taken an assignment of a lease, and in 1984 they in turn assigned the lease on. The landlord's interest was also transferred, and in February 1985 the then landlord and tenant executed a deed of variation of the terms of the lease which substantially increased the rent, made it payable in advance, rather than in arrear, and altered the covenants as to user and alienation. In 1988 both the landlord's and the tenant's interests were again transferred, and as a consequence Friends Provident became the landlord. By June 1993 the ultimate assignee had defaulted on four quarterly rent payments and was in arrears to the amount of over £30,000. Shortly after that it went into liquidation.

Friends Provident sought to enforce payment of the rent against British Railways Board, contending that they were bound by the covenant to pay the increased rent under the 1985 deed, or alternatively to pay the original rent. (As it was a pre-1996 lease, the old privity of contract regime applied, not the scheme introduced by the *Landlord and Tenant (Covenants) Act 1995*). British Railways Board argued that the 1985 deed of variation had effected a surrender and regrant, as the leasehold estate had "*significantly different incidents*" as a result. If the lease had been surrendered, it followed that their liability had been brought to an end in 1985.

The court quoted with approval from *Jenkin R Lewis & Son v Kerman [1970] 3 All ER 414*, where Russell LJ said:

> "… *even if there is no express grant of a new lease, the old lease will be surrendered by operation of law, if the arrangements made between the landlord and the tenant are such as can only be carried*

*out so as to achieve the result which they have in mind, if a new
tenancy is in fact created*

*If, for example, a tenant holds a lease of land for 20 years and he and
his landlord wish the period of his right to hold the land to be
extended by a further 20 years, their object can be achieved by the
landlord granting the tenant a reversionary lease to take effect on the
expiry of the existing lease, but if they wish a single term for the
extended period to come into being, that result can only be achieved if
the existing term is surrendered and a new term is created. It is not
possible simply to convert the existing estate in the land into a different estate by adding more years to it, and even if the parties use
words which indicate that this is what they wished to achieve the law
will achieve the result at which they are aiming in the only way in
which it can, namely by implying a fresh lease for the longer period
and a surrender of the old lease.*

*Again, if the parties wish further adjoining land to be added to the
existing holding and the rent to be increased, the transaction can, of
course, be carried out by means of a separate lease of this fresh land at
a separate rent. But if they wish there to be a single lease of all the
land at an aggregate rent, the transaction may well amount in law to
the granting of a new lease preceded by a surrender by operation of
law of the old.”*

The court in *Friends Provident* considered that the two examples
quoted, extension of the term and extension of the demise, represented
the only instances of a lease variation which would necessitate an
implied surrender and regrant.

Since neither of those things had been provided for in the deed of variation, it followed that there had been no surrender and regrant on the
facts of the case, and British Railways Board was therefore not released
from liability.

It is clear therefore that there will have been a surrender and regrant
where there has been either (a) an increase in the extent of the property

comprised in the lease, or (b) an increase in the length of the lease term. In the context of landlord's consents, this issue is likely to be raised only by a consent to works outside the demise, where it may be arguable that the arrangement operates to extend the demise. Where there has been a surrender and regrant, it is the surrender aspect which will concern landlords. The consequences would include:

- Any guarantors, or former tenants and their guarantors, remaining liable on the lease prior to variation, would be released by the surrender. This would apply to either a conventional lease guarantee, typically given by a parent company or director, or an AGA given by a previous tenant.

- If the surrendered lease was contracted out of the *Landlord and Tenant Act 1954*, that status would not apply to the new lease, except in the unlikely eventuality that the contracting-out procedure had been followed in documenting the variation. Thus the tenant would acquire security of tenure.

- If the lease was a pre-1996 lease, the benefit of the advantageous privity of contract rules applying to it would be lost, and the scheme under the *Landlord and Tenant (Covenants) Act 1995* would apply to the new lease.

Variations and former tenants/guarantors

As just noted, the issue of surrender and regrant is likely to arise in the context of landlord's consents only where permission is given for work outside the demise, thereby arguably extending it. Other consents, for matters absolutely prohibited by the lease and therefore potentially taking effect as variations of it, may not amount to a surrender and regrant, but still give rise to problems as regards the continuing liability of guarantors. The rules differ as between (a) the current tenant's guarantor, and (b) former tenants and their guarantors. The difference does not reflect any underlying policy considerations, simply a different legal analysis in each case.

Current tenant's guarantor

In the absence of express provisions in the guarantee clause, a change in the tenant's obligations under the lease will completely release the current tenant's guarantor unless either:

- the guarantor consents to the variation; or

- the variation is patently insubstantial or incapable of adversely affecting the guarantor.

This is the rule in *Holme v Brunskill (1878) 3 QBD 495 (CA)*. The case is an old one, and deals with a rather picturesque set of facts which has little to do with modern commercial leases. The case is still very much or relevance, though, and probably represents the biggest trap arising out of unintended lease variations. It concerned a yearly periodic tenancy of a farm, including a flock of 700 sheep. The defendant guaranteed that at the end of the tenancy the flock would be returned to the landlord in good condition. In settlement of a dispute over a purported notice to quit, the tenant agreed to surrender one field to the landlord, and in return the rent would be reduced and the notice to quit withdrawn. (In passing, it may be noted that a reduction in size of the demised premises, rather than an increase, does not in itself amount to a surrender and regrant). When the landlord later gave the tenant a valid notice to quit, and the tenant vacated, it was found that the flock was reduced in number and had deteriorated in quality and value, and the landlord sued the guarantor.

The case report is a short one, and not explicit as to the practical issue caused by the variation of the tenancy, though perhaps it is obvious enough: it becomes significantly harder to maintain a flock of a specified size in good condition on a reduced area of ground. The court found that the guarantee contract entered into with the defendant was to the effect that the flock should be delivered up in good condition, together with the farm as originally demised to the tenant. The guarantor ought to have been asked to decide whether he would agree to the variation in the terms of the letting and, not having been asked, he was discharged from liability. In the words of Cotton LJ:

> "*The true rule in my opinion is that if there is any agreement between the principals with reference to the contract guaranteed, the surety ought to be consulted, and that if he has not consented to the alteration, although in cases where it is without inquiry evident that the alteration is unsubstantial or that it cannot be otherwise than beneficial to the surety, the surety may not be discharged: yet, that if it is not self-evident that the alteration is unsubstantial or one which cannot be prejudicial to the surety the court ... will hold that in such a case the surety himself must be the sole judge whether or not he will consent to remain liable notwithstanding the alteration, and that if he has not so consented, he will be discharged.*"

In other words, in giving a guarantee, the guarantor does not present landlord and tenant with a blank cheque, enabling them to increase his risk without reference to him, by varying the lease.

While a guarantor will not be released from its obligations by a variation in the lease which is not prejudicial, it is clear from the quotation above that the court does not examine whether in fact there is actual prejudice or damage: it must be self-evident that this is not the case, or that the change is not substantial. The burden of showing 'no prejudice' is on the landlord trying to enforce the guarantee.

The effect of *Holme v Brunskill* can be avoided by appropriate contractual provision, and it is common to see 'anti-*Holme v Brunskill*' or 'anti-discharge' wording in a lease, typically to the effect that the giving of time to the tenant, or the variation of the lease, or any other event which would otherwise discharge the guarantor, should not do so. While a landlord should certainly insist upon such provision, the cases show that the courts interpret such wording against the landlord and in favour of the guarantor, and it cannot necessarily be relied upon.

In *Howard de Walden Estates Ltd v Pasta Place Ltd [1995] 1 EGLR 79*, a landlord's agreement that a tenant could place tables on the pavement outside a restaurant (thereby increasing the rental value of the restaurant) was held to release the guarantor. The anti-discharge provision was as follows:

> "*it is hereby agreed that any neglect or forbearance of the landlord in endeavour to obtain payment of the rents hereby reserved when the same become payable or to enforce performance of the said covenants and obligations on the part of the tenant herein or any deed or documents supplemental hereto contained at any time which may be given whether to the tenant by the landlord or the landlord by the tenant shall not release or exonerate or in any way affect the liability of the surety under this covenant*".

The court took the view that the purpose of this wording was to give the landlord a wide discretion in the case of any breach of covenant, or apprehended breach of covenant, or apprehended failure to pay rent. It should not be interpreted so as to fix the guarantor with an increased potential rental liability by means of granting licences.

In *West Horndon Industrial Park Ltd v Phoenix Timber Group Plc [1995] 1 EGLR 77*, a licence to assign gave a right to the landlord to carry out certain works of improvement to the premises, which was plainly a variation of the lease terms. The improvements to the premises would have the effect of (a) inflating the rent upon review, (b) increasing the insurance premiums payable by the tenant, and (c) making the tenant's repairing obligations more onerous. The guarantee contained 'saving wording, preserving the benefit of the guarantee:

> "... *notwithstanding any indulgence granted by the landlord to the tenant or that this lease may have been assigned or the tenant may have ceased to exist or any other act or thing whereby but for this provision the guarantor would have been released...*"

That did not apply with sufficient clarity to lease variations. The judge was clear that the provision was:

> "...not, in my view, intended to be, nor is it, a complete carte blanche to entitle the landlord to extract every and any additional burden from the surety. If it were so intended that any such additional burden should be extractable from the surety then, in my judgment, it was necessary so to have provided either expressly or by some clearer implication than is afforded by those concluding words."

Even where the lease contains saving wording of this sort, therefore, a more reliable way of avoiding the release of guarantors is to obtain their agreement to any variation. If the variation is one which arises as a consequence of a landlord's consent, then obtaining the agreement of the guarantor should be made a condition of the grant of consent.

Former tenants and their guarantors

The difference as regards former tenants and their guarantors is that while a change to the tenant's obligations cannot increase their liability, it will not completely release them in the same way as it would a current guarantor.

As regards the common law position before the *Landlord and Tenant (Covenants) Act 1995*, in *Friends Provident Life Office v British Railways Board [1995] 2 EGLR 55* the court, having decided that there had been no surrender and regrant so as to release British Railways Board from liability completely, went on to consider the effect of the deed of variation upon the extent of the liability. (It will be recalled that the deed of variation substantially increased the rent, made it payable in advance, and altered the covenants as to user and alienation).

Beldam LJ referred to:

> "the conventional distinction between the contractual liability of the lessee under his personal covenants and the liability of the assignee for the obligations of the covenants 'imprinted' on the legal estate",

going on to say:

> *"In principle therefore it is difficult to see how obligations accepted by the lessee in his contract with the lessor can be varied or increased by a subsequent agreement made by the lessor with the assignee."*

In other words, pre-1996, if an assignee agreed variations to a lease:

- The *assignee* would be bound to the varied terms by both privity of contract and privity of estate, while the lease was vested in it, and after that only by privity of contract.

- The same would apply to subsequent assignees.

- The *previous tenant*, though, could not be affected under privity of estate, having already assigned the lease before the variation; and while it would remain bound to the landlord by privity of contract, its obligations under that contract were those of the unvaried lease. Those obligations could not be varied without the agreement of the previous tenant.

The rule is therefore that that the obligations of former tenants (and by extension their guarantors) will remain subsisting, but cannot be made more onerous by an agreement made between the landlord and any assignee.

That is the position as regards variations made prior to 1996. For variations made post-1995, the position is governed by *s.18, Landlord and Tenant (Covenants) Act 1995*. This is one of three sections in the Act, *ss.17-19*, which apply both to old and to new tenancies, so the applicability of *s.18* depends on the date of the variation, not the date of the lease.

- *s.17* requires notice to be served on any former tenant or their guarantor (not the current tenant's guarantor) within six months of any sum falling due under the lease, as a condition of recovering the sum from them.

- *s.19* entitles a recipient of a s.17 notice, who has paid the sums detailed in it, to an overriding lease of the property.

- Under *s.18*, in addition to any common law rule whereby a guarantor may be released from liability by a variation of the lease (i.e. the rule in *Holme v Brunskill*), it is provided that any recipient of a s.17 notice, whether former tenant or guarantor, is not liable to pay any amount detailed in the notice, to the extent that the amount is referable to the variation. That is subject to an exception where a guarantor has consented to the variation.

Thus the rule is similar for pre-1996 and post-1995 variations. 'Similar' because while on the face of it no real difference is apparent, the pre-1996 position is governed by the common law, while the post-1995 rule is statutory. Points of statutory interpretation may in due course arise which expose differences; this has not happened yet.

The inability to increase the liability of a former tenant or its guarantor is clearly a less serious matter for the landlord than the complete release of a current guarantor by the operation of the rule in *Holme v Brunskill*. Nevertheless it will be preferable to be able to have recourse against former tenants and their guarantors on the basis of the lease terms as varied, where possible. That means obtaining their agreement to whatever variation may be involved, although in practical terms it may be difficult to persuade a party with no further involvement in a property that there is anything in it for them in co-operating in this way.

Be alert to lease variations

As appears from the above, there will be no total release of a current tenant's guarantor, or limitation on the liability of a former tenant or their guarantor, if that party has consented to the variation. Well-advised landlords will have ensured that all relevant consents were obtained from those parties whenever a lease has been varied.

However, there is a potential danger here, in that consideration of the implications as regards guarantors and former tenants may be prompted only when dealing with deeds of variation so-called. If dealing with something called a 'licence to alter', 'licence to change use', or 'licence to share occupation', the risks may be overlooked.

This seems to be precisely what happened in *Topland Portfolio No 1 Ltd v Smiths News Trading Ltd [2014] EWCA Civ 18*, mentioned at the beginning of the chapter. It will be recalled that the landlord consented to certain works by means of a 'licence to alter', although the court subsequently held that a variation to the lease had been effected, because the works consented to were otherwise the subject of an absolute prohibition under the lease.

The tenant was Do-it-All, which was a joint venture company partly owned by WH Smith, which had provided a guarantee from its parent company, Smiths News Trading Ltd. The lease contained the usual tenant's obligation to repair the demised premises, and defined 'the demised premises' to include alterations and additions. It also attempted to exclude the impact of *Holme v Brunskill* by providing that the guarantor should not be released by any "*neglect or forbearance*" of the landlord in enforcing the lease covenants.

The lease was a pre-1996 one, so the old privity of contract rules applied. The licence to alter was issued in 1987, and the guarantor's consent was not sought or obtained, probably because it was regarded as a matter of landlord's consent, and not a lease variation.

Topland subsequently became the landlord. When the then tenant became insolvent, in 2012, Topland sued the guarantor. The guarantor argued that it was not liable, having been released by the rule in *Holme v Brunskill* because the previous landlord had allowed the tenant to carry out works that were absolutely prohibited by the lease. (Although at the time of the claim it was a former tenant's guarantor, at the time the licence to alter was issued it was the current guarantor, so the position was governed by *Holme v Brunskill*). This argument succeeded, and the court dismissed the claim.

The increase in the bulk of structures on the land meant that there would inevitably be an increase in the burden of repairing obligations on the tenant, which in turn would increase the exposure of the guarantor. Accordingly, far from it being self-evident that there was no prejudice to the guarantor as a result of the variation, the opposite was true.

The attempt to exclude the *Holme v Brunskill* rule was ineffective, since the issuing of the licence was more than "*neglect or forbearance*". The case provides another example of the way in which the courts construe these clauses against landlords.

The lesson is to be alive to the possibility of concealed variations when documenting a landlord's consent. More specifically, when presented with a tenant's application for consent to alterations, and the accompanying schedule of proposed works, it can be difficult for a landlord to be certain whether all of those works are within the demise, or the subject of a prohibition under the lease which is not absolute but fully qualified. The prudent approach is to ensure that the consent of any guarantor is always obtained whenever the landlord grants licence for alterations, regardless of the circumstances.

It is striking that the guarantor in this case was able to avoid liability on the basis of a licence to alter entered into 25 years previously, the significance of which had not been appreciated until such time as the claim was brought. Any guarantor, former tenant, or former tenant's guarantor, faced with a claim in the event of default by the current tenant, is well-advised to consider the title documents closely, paying particular attention to any licences.

Summary

What appears to be a matter of a landlord's consent can actually amount to variation of the lease, if what the landlord is consenting to goes beyond the contractual framework of the lease. This may be where the landlord consents to work which extends beyond the demised premises, or it may be where the landlord consents to some action which is the subject of an absolute prohibition in the lease.

Where alterations are to be effected by the tenant beyond the demise, a possible analysis is that the variation of the lease thus effected will result in the demise being enlarged. In that case, the lease will be impliedly surrendered by operation of law, and a new lease of the enlarged demise will have been granted in its place. The surrender thus effected will release the obligations of all guarantors and former tenants remaining liable on the lease covenants, and cancel out any contracting-out of the lease.

Variations which fall short of effecting a surrender and regrant may still have significant effects.

- A current guarantor will be released from any obligations at all by a variation to the lease to which it has not agreed, unless either (a) the variation self-evidently cannot be prejudicial to it, or (b) there is effective wording in the lease to exclude this rule. Neither possibility affords a landlord reliable assistance, and it is better to insist upon the guarantor agreeing to any variation.

- A former tenant or its guarantor will not be released by a variation of the lease, but the variation cannot increase their liability. The exception to this is where that party has agreed to the variation, but there is often no incentive for them to agree to it.

It is therefore important to be alert to the possibility that a landlord's consent may take effect as a variation of the lease. In practice, this is particularly likely in the case of consent to alterations, and a good rule is to insist upon the guarantor being a party to any licence to alter.

CHAPTER EIGHT
DOCUMENTING LEASE
VARIATIONS

This chapter deals with ways of documenting lease variations, and the required formalities. It covers express surrender and regrant, deeds of variation, side letters, and adding to the demise by means of a supplemental lease.

It is to be hoped that landlord and tenant will, for the most part, recognise when the arrangement they wish to document constitutes a variation of the lease terms rather than just a consent, and that the documentation will accordingly take the appropriate form.

Express surrender and regrant

Surrender and regrant does not only happen by accident. If the parties recognise that they propose to vary the lease in a way which means that an implied surrender and regrant is a possibility, then an express, intentional surrender enables planning for the consequences outlined in the previous chapter. The new lease can be the subject of a straightforward contracting-out, if required; new guarantees can be negotiated, to replace any lost as a result of the surrender; and SDLT liability can be anticipated and budgeted for. The only consequence that cannot be avoided is that the new lease will necessarily be entered into post-1995, and will therefore be one to which the *Landlord and Tenant (Covenants) Act 1995* applies.

The Land Registry's requirements for registering a surrender by operation of law are set out in *section 5* of *Practice Guide 26*. Generally, the Land Registry may require a statutory declaration or statement of truth to outline the facts that led to the surrender.

However, one occasion on which this is not necessary is where the landlord grants a new lease of the same premises to the existing tenant.

As explained earlier, the essence of implied surrender and regrant is that a new lease is granted to a person in respect of premises of which that person is already the tenant. This may be something which is done with the acknowledged intention of effecting a surrender of the first lease. Where this is done, it is not necessary to document the surrender, which will happen automatically as a matter of law. However, in that case the Land Registry does require a letter from either the landlord or the tenant (or their solicitors) to confirm that no deed of surrender was entered into.

Alternatively, the parties may choose to enter into a deed of surrender, as well as a new lease, and in that case also no statutory declaration or statement of truth is necessary.

In the context of landlord's consents, it will principally be where the proposed consent involves adding to the demise that an express surrender and regrant will be worth considering.

Deed of variation

Where a surrender and regrant is neither necessary nor desirable, the obvious mechanism is a deed of variation. Since a variation involves an alteration by way of contract of the contractual relations between the parties, the agreement for variation must itself possess the characteristics of a valid contract. Therefore, the agreement for variation must be supported by consideration or made by deed.

At common law, a contract made by deed could only be varied by a deed (*West v Blakeway (1841) 2 Man & G 729*). In modern law , a contract made by deed may be varied by written agreement. This is the equitable rule and now prevails by virtue of the *Senior Courts Act 1981 s 49(1)*: see *Berry v Berry [1929] 2 KB 316*.

The requirement for writing applies whether or not the lease was made by deed, since the lease must be in writing by virtue of *s.2, Law of*

Property (Miscellaneous Provisions) Act 1989, and therefore so must any variation: *Record v Bell [1991] 1 WLR 853*.

Where either of the lease and the reversion are registered, any variation will need to be completed by registration against the titles of the landlord and the tenant. Guidance is contained in the Land Registry's *Practice Guide 25*.

In the case of an unregistered lease or reversion, it is good practice to endorse a memorandum on the lease and counterpart, to record the variation.

Side letters

Parties to a lease may sometimes vary the obligations under a lease by means of a 'side letter'. This may be because the intention is not to vary the lease, but only to effect a concession which is personal to the parties. This would plainly be an inappropriate way of documenting any arrangement which might amount to an addition to the demise, for instance, and side letters tend to be used for matters such as relaxing the alienation covenant, or the user covenant, or departing from the insurance arrangements envisaged by the lease.

If the concession is personal to the tenant, then there will be a question as to whether a successor in title to the landlord will be bound in the event that the reversion is sold. The same issue would arise the other way round, in the event of concessions personal to the landlord, when the lease is assigned (it is unusual to encounter concessions granted by tenants in favour of landlords, however). When drafting a side letter, it is therefore important to specify the intended effect upon the successors of each of the original parties.

If it is silent on the point, then successors may be bound. The position differs depending upon whether the lease is an 'old' lease or a 'new' lease for the purposes of the *Landlord and Tenant (Covenants) Act 1995*.

'Old' leases – *s.142, Law of Property Act 1925*

In *System Floors Ltd v Ruralpride Ltd [1995] 1 EGLR 48*, the Court of Appeal was satisfied that a side letter expressed as personal to the tenant (but silent with regard to the landlord's successors) bound the landlord's successor, even though they did not know of the side letter when they acquired the freehold. The letter gave the tenant the right to require the landlord for the time being to accept the surrender of the leases, and the right to sub-let, and also exempted the tenant from liability for certain repairs. The successor landlord was bound because the obligations in the side letter fell within *s.142, Law of Property Act 1925*, which provides that the burden of covenants that have "*reference to the subject matter of the lease*" (i.e. touch and concern the land) automatically pass to any purchaser of the reversion. The transmission of the burden of the covenant was not dependent on the transmission of the benefit. Therefore, the fact that the letter was expressed as personal to the tenant did not prevent the obligations binding the landlord's successors.

In *Lotteryking v AMEC Properties [1995] 2 EGLR 13*, the court confirmed that for *s.142* to apply the side letter does not need to take the form of a deed.

Note that *s.142* does not apply to post-1995 leases: *s.30(4), Landlord and Tenant (Covenants) Act 1995*.

This potential to bind successors applies to concessions in favour of tenants. If a tenant were to enter into a concessionary arrangement in favour of the landlord, and personal to the landlord, there is no provision equivalent to *s.142* which would bind the tenant's assignees. It would be most unusual to encounter such an arrangement, however.

'New' leases – *Landlord and Tenant (Covenants) Act 1995*

Under the 1995 Act the position is rather more straightforward:

- a covenant includes a collateral agreement (*s.28*);

- a collateral agreement means an agreement collateral to the tenancy, whether made before or after the creation of the tenancy and regardless of whether it touches and concerns the land (*ss.2(1)* and *28(1)*); and

- the benefit and burden of covenants are annexed to the relevant interest and will automatically pass to the assignee of the lease or the reversion (*s.3(1)*) unless the covenant is expressed to be personal (*s.3(6)*).

Variations contained in side letters will therefore bind successors in title, whether landlord or tenant, unless expressly personal in nature.

Adding to the demise: supplemental leases

Where there is a danger of implied surrender and regrant, the options are not limited to express surrender and regrant and deed of variation. If the arrangement to be documented involves extending the demise, another option is to grant a new lease of the additional space, on all the same terms as the existing lease, to stand alongside it.

An attraction of doing this is that where a new lease is being granted that is in identical or very similar terms to an existing one, it is not necessary to prepare an entirely new full-length document. The supplemental lease can instead be in short form, stating that the letting is on the same terms as the lease of the original premises except in certain respects, which will be set out in the supplemental lease, normally in a schedule.

The obvious differences are the length of the term, the amount of the rent and the description of the premises. It is likely that all the remaining terms of the lease will remain the same.

It will still be necessary for any SDLT on the new lease to be calculated and paid, and to register the lease (and any easements) at the Land

Registry. A supplemental lease is no different from any other lease in those respects.

Joining premises together

Where this solution becomes complicated is in circumstances where the tenant will be physically joining together the two sets of premises demised by the original lease and the supplemental lease. (This situation is perhaps unlikely to arise in the context of an application for consent, but is addressed here for completeness).

- In such a case, the landlord will be keen to ensure that the tenant is not able to assign the new lease without also assigning the old lease, and *vice versa*. In order to achieve this, it is necessary to vary the existing lease, to include a tenant's covenant not to assign the existing lease without also assigning the new lease. This will need a deed of variation for the existing lease, as well as a supplemental lease.

- The works would need to be documented by way of a licence to alter, and there would almost always be a need to ensure that a requirement to reinstate was either included in the licence to alter, or present in both leases. The works might have a structural element, so if the existing lease has an absolute prohibition on structural works, the 'licence to alter' might take effect as a deed of variation.

- It is possible to include any variation of the existing lease as a pro-vision in the supplemental lease, though regardless of which document effects the variation it is important to be mindful of the potential for guarantors to be released from their liability by any variation to which they are not party, and to ensure that they join in the documentation.

- To avoid any suggestion of an implied surrender and regrant, there would be separate rent reviews under each lease (assuming the term to be of sufficient length) and this raises two issues. First, it will usually be appropriate to provide for the valuation to disregard any effect on rent of alterations carried out to unite the two sets of premises. Secondly, in relation to each review, the tenant will be a 'special bidder', since a higher rental bid must be expected from the tenant of adjoining, conjoined premises. Whether the 'special bid' should be disregarded for valuation purposes will be a matter for negotiation between the landlord and the tenant.

Because of all these issues, where two sets of premises are to be joined together, it is almost always easier to effect an express surrender and regrant.

Summary

An express surrender and regrant may be a sensible option in the event of variations which amount to an extension of the demise. Otherwise, variations are likely to be documented by a deed of variation.

Where a lease will explicitly be varied, the variation must be in writing, and either supported by consideration or made by deed. If either the lease or the landlord's title are registered, the appropriate Land Registry requirements must be complied with. If unregistered, a memorandum of the variation should be endorsed on the lease and counterpart.

If a variation is intended to take effect as a concession which is personal to one party, usually the tenant, it is useful to provide expressly whether successors in title to the other party will be bound. If there is no provision, then successors may be bound, under the general law.

A further option for documenting which adds to the demise is to grant a supplemental lease. This is not without some difficulties, particularly where the two sets of premises are to be physically joined together.

CHAPTER NINE
CONDUCT OF APPLICATIONS –
ASSIGNMENT AND SUB-LETTING

This chapter and the next consider the conduct of applications for landlord's consent, by both landlord and tenant. In this chapter, applications in relation to assignment and sub-letting are considered, while the next deals with alterations. The next chapter also discusses the risks of informal consents, which is an issue common to all types of application. This chapter addresses the formalities for making an application, and the time constraints upon the landlord issuing its decision. The provisions of the *Alienation Protocol* are discussed, together with the typical content of licence deeds.

Consideration of what is reasonable is not confined to the substance of the landlord's answer to the tenant's application. The conduct of the application is brought into question too, since the usual form of words is that landlord's consent is not to be "*unreasonably withheld or delayed*" (emphasis supplied). As regards assignment and sub-letting, the *Landlord and Tenant Act 1988* applies, of course, and there is a statutory duty to make a decision on the tenant's application "*within a reasonable time*".

When applications for landlord's consent to assignment or sub-letting become contentious, it is very often the case that the tenant complains of unreasonable delay by the landlord. Putting pressure on the landlord to make its decision promptly, whatever it may be, tends to be regarded by tenants as extra leverage to obtain a decision which is positive. If the landlord is not confident of its reason for objection, that is probably a sound instinct. In any event, the upshot is that the caselaw on what is a reasonable time to make the decision is well developed.

That in turn has consequences for what is best practice in conducting applications (whether for the landlord or the tenant), and the *Alienation Protocol* has useful content on this. There are other issues to be aware of in relation to the conduct of applications, but timing is the most important one.

Starting the clock

It is obvious enough that the calculation of the reasonable time must begin from the time when an application is made. In the context of alienation, though, this has a technical meaning.

Under *s.1(3)* of the 1988 Act the statutory duties arise:

> *"where there is served upon the person who may consent to a proposed transaction a written application by the tenant".*

A preliminary consideration is that initial correspondence is not always in terms that make it abundantly clear whether the tenant is applying for consent or not. For instance, a tenant might write an exploratory letter to the landlord, sounding out whether a particular user would be acceptable. If the letter also included information on the identity of the tenant, and whether an assignment or sub-letting was proposed, it might not be easy to tell whether it was an application under *s.1(3)*. The landlord might consider asking for confirmation as to whether the tenant intended to make an actual application, though there is a judgment to be made about whether that is helpful or not. If the application process was expected to be difficult, with the question of timing likely to feature, it could be worthwhile delaying that query for a while, to give room to argue that the clock started running later than the tenant might believe. As ever, it will depend on the circumstances.

Assuming a communication which is unmistakably intended as an application, though, the next issue is whether that communication has been *"served"* in accordance with the meaning of *s.1(3)*.

Service under the 1988 Act is provided for in *s.5(2)* which states that:

> *"An application or notice is to be treated as served for the purposes of this Act if (a) served in any manner provided in the tenancy, and (b) in respect of any matter for which the tenancy makes no provision, served in any manner provided by section 23, Landlord and Tenant Act 1927."*

Whether an application had been validly served was at issue in *E.ON UK PLC v Gilesports Ltd [2012] 3 EGLR 23*. The lease in that case provided that *s.196, Law of Property Act 1925* should apply in relation to serving notices. An application for consent to assign was made by e-mail to the landlord's managing agent, which was not in accordance with the methods of service provided for in *s.196* (or for the matter of that *s.23* of the 1927 Act). It was held that the application for consent had not been validly served, and accordingly there could be no question of unreasonable delay. Time had not begun to run, and indeed none of the statutory duties under the Act had arisen.

The decision is open to criticism:

- It proceeded upon the agreed basis that the application should have been served in accordance with *s.196*, however the lease made provision for *notices* to be served in accordance with that section, not *applications*. It is at least arguable that the relevant service regime was the fall-back option provided for in *s.5(2)*, namely that under *s.23, Landlord and Tenant Act 1927*.

- As regards *s.23*, it has been held in *Galinski v McHugh [1989] 1 EGLR 109* that *s.23* does not preclude service being effected by a method not provided for in that section; the section is, in the judicial terminology, 'directory' not 'mandatory'. It is generally considered that the same applies to *s.196*. The judge in *E.ON v Gilesports* rejected that proposition, but without discussion or authority. It is still arguable that service by other methods is not excluded by *s.196*. The e-mail application may therefore have been sufficiently served, whichever of the two statutory regimes applied. (It is true that there is some debate over whether documents can validly be served by e-mail, since it is not clear that it can be regarded as 'writing'. While there is no decision of general application on the point, the Law Commission has opined that e-mail should be regarded as 'writing', and so capable of amounting to good service.)

Nevertheless, a prudent tenant will serve its application in accordance with the lease provisions applying to service of notices (some modern leases make provision specifically for service of applications as well), or if there are none, in accordance with *s.23*.

Of course, should it emerge in the course of a dispute that no application had been served in accordance with *s.5(2)* of the 1988 Act, the defect is easily remedied by serving one in the required way. The time for considering the application would only then begin to run, but against the context of previous discussions and correspondence, it could be expected to be very short. There could be costs implications, however, and it is a situation which is easily avoided by getting it right in the first place.

One other point as to the start of the 'reasonable time' is to do with applications made with incomplete information. The landlord will need information as to what it is being asked to consent to. The tenant should anticipate the information the landlord will require, and provide it together with the application. But if an application is made, even without some important information, it will still start the clock running (*Norwich Union v Mercantile Credit [2003] EWHC 3064 (Ch)*, and *Lombard North Central v Remax Herbane [2008] EWHC 316 (Ch)*). However, late provision of essential information would naturally be relevant to the assessment of whether the landlord had given its decision with a reasonable time.

Costs can also be a complicating factor at this initial stage. Since it will generally be reasonable to require an undertaking as to costs (*Dong Bang Minerva (UK) Ltd v Davina Ltd [1996] 2 EGLR 31*), does it follow that the reasonable time is not running until such time as an undertaking has been provided? The point was left open in *Dong Bang*, though in practice landlords always refuse to deal with the matter until an undertaking has been given. The decision in *No 1 West India Quay (Residential) Ltd v East Tower Apartments Ltd [2016] EWHC 2438 (Ch)* suggests that the landlord's refusal to consider the application until the required on-account payment of costs had been made was unreasonable; it is not altogether clear, though, whether it was that or the failure to justify the amount demanded which made the requirement unreasonable. It is possible that time runs despite a failure to provide security as to costs, but the current caselaw leaves the point open.

The *Alienation Protocol* suggests that a landlord who considers that insufficient security for costs has been given, and who proposes to suspend dealing with the application on that account, should give the tenant its reasons promptly. It also states that a landlord should not use costs as an excuse to delay dealing with a matter, and cautions that to do may be unreasonable. Where an undertaking for a certain figure has been given, or an on-account payment made, and it becomes apparent that the figure will be exceeded, the *Alienation Protocol* states that the landlord should not suspend progressing the application while the matter of costs is renegotiated, but continue up until the initial figure is reached.

What is a reasonable time?

General approach

The judgment of Munby J in *Go West v Spigarolo [2003] EWCA Civ 17* contains a comment which is a useful pointer in general terms:

> *"It may be that the reasonable time referred to in section 1(3) will sometimes have to be measured in weeks rather than days; but even in complicated cases, it should in my view be measured in weeks rather than months"*

There is a commonly encountered view that, as a rule of thumb, 28 days can be regarded as reasonable in the usual case. (This perhaps harks back to the Law Commission's original proposal for a 28-day period, in its report *No. 141, 'Covenants Restricting, Dispositions, Alterations and Change of User').* The *Alienation Protocol* provides that the landlord should aim to communicate its decision in writing within 21 days, but it also acknowledges that what is reasonable must always be a question of fact in the particular circumstances. The latter proposition is the starting-point, and any alleged rule of thumb must be treated with a great deal of caution.

The *Alienation Protocol* provides a list of factors which are likely to be relevant in the assessment of a reasonable time in any particular case:

- The type and amount of information provided to, and requested by, the landlord;

- The speed with which the tenant responds to requests for information;

- Any particular urgency or time limit constraining the tenant, which has been notified to the landlord;

- The complexity of the transaction, corporate structure and any guarantee arrangements, and the complexity of any unusual legal and estate management issues to be dealt with by the landlord when making its decision; and

- Whether the tenant is likely to suffer loss as a result of a delay.

Of course, the list can never be exhaustive.

The first two items on the list are of great practical importance. Any delay by the tenant in providing information can have an impact on assessing the overall reasonable time for dealing with an application. Equally, the landlord cannot point to the length of time taken to obtain information as an excusing factor, if it has itself contributed to the delay by being slow in requesting information.

Provision of information

The *Alienation Protocol* also contains a useful list of the sort of information which is generally expected. Certain of the items on that list have been outlined previously, but it is helpful to see the list in full:

- The application should specify the nature of the transaction and identify the assignee/sub-tenant, together with any guarantor.

- It should include sufficient information about the assignee/sub-tenant (and any guarantor), including:

  - A description of their trade or business

  - Registered number and office, in the case of companies

  - In the case of individuals, references or referees' contact details

- It should provide details of the proposed use of the premises.

- It should include an offer to meet the landlord's proper and reasonable costs of the application.

- It should explain any circumstances of particular urgency.

- In the case of an application for consent to sub-let, it should be accompanied by a draft sub-lease, or at least detailed heads of terms.

- In the case of an application for consent to assign, the information on the assignee should include information demonstrating that the assignee (and any guarantor) will be able to comply with the lease obligations. This may include the last three years' accounts, or a business plan with profit forecasts.

It should be borne in mind that of course there may be related applications, for consent to alterations, perhaps also change of use, and information will need to be supplied for the purposes of those applications as well. They will be separate applications, and delay by the tenant in providing information on the alterations will not excuse delay by the landlord in dealing with the alienation aspect, in breach of its statutory duties under the 1988 Act. Nevertheless, in practical terms the transaction cannot proceed until all consents have been obtained, so the tenant needs to assemble all relevant information on those matters as well.

Ideally a tenant would supply all the information together with the application, in a single package, rather than having it emerge piecemeal. All too often, incomplete information is given at the outset, and the full picture emerges only over a period of weeks or even months. Ideally, too, the landlord would respond promptly to an application with a full and considered 'shopping list' of any further information required, rather than realising after several weeks that it would be useful to see the assignee's business plan.

The *Alienation Protocol* recommends that identification by the landlord of any further required information, and provision of that information by the tenant, should be orderly and prompt. Specifically, the landlord should be listing out the required further information within five working days of receiving the application, so far as it can. The tenant should be providing the information requested as soon as reasonably possible. Both the request and the additional information should come as single packages, rather than piecemeal.

The intention is of course to set out best practice, and in the real world there are many things that can get in the way.

- The bulk of the information relates to the assignee or sub-tenant, but the landlord's line of communication is with the tenant. The ability to provide the information promptly and in one package may therefore be hampered.

- Also, some of the information might just be unavailable until a later stage. If the application is for consent to sub-letting, the agreed form of the sub-lease will be a very important piece of information, but that may still be in negotiation at the time of the application.

- The landlord may be reliant on advice from professionals; for example, if three years' accounts are provided, the landlord will usually refer that information either to its surveyors or to accountants. They may report that they are not satisfied with the financial status as disclosed by the accounts, and require a copy of a current business plan, or some other information, but getting that advice could quite easily take more than the five working days which the *Alienation Protocol* envisages.

Another potential issue, of course, is whether it is reasonable to require a particular piece of information. There is a risk for the landlord that the court might regard the request as just an attempt to be obstructive. That was the court's conclusion in *Design Progression Ltd v Thurloe Properties Ltd [2004] EWHC 324 (Ch)*, where the landlord had been supplied with very full financial information on the assignee, but attempted to insist on further information as to its trade debtors and creditors.

The process of providing and requesting information can lead the landlord and its advisors into regarding the reasonable time as something which can be extended by means of a purely arithmetical exercise, thus:

- The length of delay attributable to the landlord is calculated, also that attributable to the tenant.

- If the tenant has delayed more than the landlord, the notional reasonable period is extended by the net amount.

Calculating how much delay has been caused by each party may be of some assistance to a court, after the event, in deciding whether there has been unreasonable delay on the landlord's part. Relying upon some notional reasonable period is, though, a risky way of guiding a landlord's actions as events unfold, as it may ignore the wider picture. For example: a landlord might actually reach its decision, say, 14 days after receiving the tenant's application, but for reasons of its own delay notifying the decision to the tenant about its decision until day 27. It cannot hope to argue successfully that it had a notional 28 days in which to decide, and has therefore complied with the statutory duty to give its decision within a reasonable time (*Mount Eden Land Ltd v Folia Ltd [2003] EWHC 1815 (Ch)*).

Circumstances of urgency

Aside from promptness, or lack of, in requesting and providing inform-ation, another factor which crops up repeatedly is that there is some particular urgency for the tenant, which has been brought to the landlord's attention. A typical scenario might be that the prospective assignee is actively considering other premises, and requires to know before some short deadline whether this deal will go ahead. The tenant will in turn attempt to impose that deadline on the landlord, and the landlord will resist the notion that the tenant can dictate the timetable. However, the assignee's deadline is a very important piece of the factual picture, and the landlord ignores it at their peril.

Of course the tenant may try to lay down an impossibly tight timetable, in which case the landlord should tell them, promptly, exactly why it's impossible. But unless it is, then the landlord should take into the account the timing constraints on the tenant. It is suggested that in practice a good approach is for the landlord to put itself in the tenant's shoes, and give the application the degree of priority which the tenant would.

Relieving time pressure

In circumstances where the tenant is putting the landlord under acute pressure as regards alleged unreasonable delay, but there remain unre-solved objections to the transaction, how can the landlord relieve the time pressure while still addressing its concerns? One possible sensible solution can be illustrated by an example.

Say a tenant sells shoes, and the lease permits any retail use, with no need for landlord's consent to change use so long as the new use is a retail one. There is a proposal to assign the lease to a retailer of drum-kits, and the landlord is concerned that noise nuisance will be caused to other neighbouring tenants. The parties have been unable to agree upon the sound-proofing measures required, and the tenant threatens a damages claim based on unreasonable delay.

The landlord can relieve the time pressure by offering a form of licence deed stipulating a condition that the assignee installs the required soundproofing measures. Then the debate becomes one which is squarely about the reasonableness or otherwise of the condition, and the timing issue goes away.

That will not always be an appropriate way forward, everything will be fact-dependent as always, but it should be borne in mind as an option.

Avoiding waiver of the right to forfeit

A particularly difficult issue can arise when the landlord is subject to the duties in *s.1(3)* of the 1988 Act, but needs to avoid waiving a right to forfeit the lease.

The right to forfeit is likely to be directly related to the application for consent. Retrospective applications for consent are irregular, in the sense that the lease will usually require landlord's "*prior*" consent, but they are not uncommon. It is frequently the case that, in a business acquisition, time does not allow for the seller to go through the process of applying for landlord's consent to assign each of the leases it holds, and dealing with each landlord's objections. Instead, the sale proceeds, including assignment of the leases (or sometimes the grant of licences to occupy by the seller, pending assignment) and consent is then applied for retrospectively. The landlord is thus presented with a breach of covenant as well as an application for consent. This can occur in cases where the tenant has gone into administration, too, as discussed in chapter 12.

Another situation which sometimes crops up might be: a tenant applies for consent to assign, and the landlord objects because it is not satisfied with the financial status of the assignee. Negotiations as to providing acceptable security ensue. Tenant and assignee both take the view that the landlord is plainly unreasonable, and that accordingly there will be no breach of covenant in simply going ahead with the assignment, which they proceed to do. From the landlord's point of view, since he believes that he is not being unreasonable, this is a breach of covenant, and gives rise to a right to forfeit.

It is a difficult position for the landlord. On the one hand, a concern about the covenant strength of the assignee is important, and the only effective remedy, if an acceptable compromise cannot be reached, is forfeiture. On the other, there are many disadvantages to forfeiture, particularly if it is not a strong letting market, and the landlord may ultimately be prepared to allow the assignment to proceed, if appropriate security can be negotiated. The landlord will want, therefore, to preserve the ability to forfeit the lease, while attempting to negotiate acceptable security.

The problem is the well-established rule that once the landlord has knowledge of the facts giving rise to a right to forfeit, any act or statement by it or on its behalf, which expressly or implicitly acknowledges the continuing existence of the lease, will be treated as a choice to allow it to continue, and so will waive the right to forfeit. This means that the landlord cannot deal with the application for consent, since it is implicit in doing so that the lease continues to exist. Even if the landlord suspends any dealing with the application, even an incautious allusion to 'your lease' risks waiver.

Ideally, the landlord would have no contact with the tenant whatsoever. However, the duties under *s.1(3)* continue to apply: the landlord must engage in the process sufficiently to establish whether its objections are reasonable, and must deliver its decision within a reasonable time. If it fails to do so, it risks a claim for damages.

There is no completely reliable way of squaring this circle. Perhaps the best the landlord can do is (a) make sure that all correspondence is 'without prejudice' (though it is not clear that this prevents waiver), and (b) explicitly limit its continuing consideration of the application to the possibility of an application for relief from forfeiture. That position might be set out like this: the landlord intends to forfeit the lease; if it does so, the landlord recognises that the tenant might make an application for relief from forfeiture, which might succeed; therefore the lease is potentially good, and purely on the basis that there might be a successful application for relief, the landlord continues to engage with the application for consent.

Other matters

There are three other short points to be made about the landlord's duty to communicate its decision within a reasonable time. The first is that consent is usually not just a matter of the landlord saying 'yes' in a letter. The consent is going to be embodied in a formal licence deed, so the time taken in the negotiation and completion of the deed should be factored in when trying to deliver the decision within a reasonable time.

The second is a point which featured in *Go West v Spigarolo*. The landlord in that case issued a refusal prematurely, but thereafter continued to negotiate the application. It subsequently argued that a reasonable time for considering the application had not yet elapsed. That argument was rejected. If a landlord refuses the tenant's application, that effectively brings to an end the period of time allowed to the landlord to make its decision. Another way of putting it is that the assessment of what might be a reasonable time may be affected by events subsequent to the application, and does not necessarily depend upon facts known only at that time; the landlord having made its decision, whether negative or positive, is highly relevant to an assessment of how long the landlord reasonably required.

Finally, it is generally assumed that 'reasonable time' is only a risk area where the landlord has not granted consent, but that might not necessarily be the case. Imagine an application for consent to assign made on 12 May. The landlord gives its consent on 12 July. In the meantime, another quarter's rent has fallen due on 24 June, payable by the tenant. A court, if called upon to do so, might conclude that it was unreasonable for the landlord to have delayed making its decision beyond 12 June. In that case, if the landlord had given its consent by 12 June, the rent due on 24 June would have been payable by the assignee, so the tenant has suffered loss as a result of the landlord's breach of its statutory duty, even though the assignment has been permitted. There is no reported case in which a tenant has claimed damages in such circumstances, successfully or otherwise, but it is at least a theoretical possibility.

Communicating the landlord's decision

There are also some important points to note about the landlord's response to the application.

Means of communicating refusal, or stipulation of conditions

The provisions of s.5(2) of the 1988 Act, dealing with the means of serving the tenant's application, also apply to service of notice of the landlord's decision. It is possible (there is no reported case on this point) that communicating the decision in a way which does not satisfy s.5(2) gives the tenant a claim on the basis of unreasonable delay, so a landlord who is giving anything other than a positive answer should consider serving it as required by s.5(2).

Reasons for the decision

If consent is refused, s.1(3)(b) requires that the reasons for the refusal are specified in the written notice. The landlord may only rely on the reasons it set out in its written refusal. Other reasons cannot be added at a later date (*Footwear Corporation v Amplight [1998] 2 EGLR 38* and *Norwich Union v Shopmoor [1998] 2 EGLR 167*).

If consent is given, but is subject to any conditions, *s.1(3)(b)* requires that those conditions are specified in the written notice. Unlike in the case of a refusal, the landlord is not required to give its reasons for any conditions. However, if the landlord does impose conditions, *s.1(6)(b)* provides that it is for the landlord to show that the conditions are reasonable. It has been held that in doing so the landlord may only rely on written reasons given to the tenant within a reasonable time of receiving the application for consent (*London & Argyll Developments v Mount Cook Land Limited [2003] All ER (D) 104 (Jun)*).

The upshot must be that a landlord who is refusing consent, or stipulating conditions, will want to be as comprehensive as possible, and to include even matters which are likely to turn out to be spurious or unreasonable, to preserve the ability to rely on them later if need be. As already discussed in Chapter 4, if a refusal letter has both bad and good reasons, the bad ones do not invalidate the good (*No.1 West India Quay (Residential) Ltd v East Tower Apartments Ltd [2018] EWCA Civ 250*).

Means of communicating positive decision

The landlord will generally want to have consent documented in a formal licence deed, which will set out the conditions for consent. Depending upon the nature of what is being consented to, the licence deed will usually address a variety of other matters too.

Typical provisions in a licence to assign the lease might include:

- An AGA (Authorised Guarantee Agreement) from the assigning tenant.

- A GAGA (Guarantee of an AGA) from the assigning tenant's guarantor.

- A guarantee from the assignee's guarantor.

- A covenant from the assignee with the landlord, to perform the lease covenants.

- Agreement from the assigning tenant, the assignor, and all guarantors to any matter which amounts to a variation of the lease, such as a change of use (if otherwise absolutely prohibited).

- Tenant's agreement not to let the assignee into occupation prior to completion.

- Where the lease is contracted-out of the *Landlord and Tenant Act 1954*, provision in relation to contracting-out of any new lease which a guarantor might be called upon to take in the event of forfeiture of disclaimer of the current lease.

- The tenant must supply the assignee with important documents such as the Environmental Performance Certificate, and asbestos survey.

- Notification of completion of the permitted assignment is to be provided to the landlord, with details of where rent demands should be sent.

- The assignee must complete Land Registry formalities.

- Time limit within which transaction is to be completed (typically three months).

Typical provisions in a licence to sub-let might include:

- Provision as to contracting-out of the sub-lease.

- Tenant's agreement not to let the sub-tenant into occupation prior to completion.

- Tenant's agreement to not to conclude any rent review under the sub-lease without the landlord's approval.

- Tenant's agreement to enforce the terms of the sub-lease, and not to waive or vary them.

- Agreement from the tenant and its guarantor, if any, to any matter which amounts to a variation of the lease, such as a change of use (if otherwise absolutely prohibited).

- Sub-tenant's agreement to complete Land Registry formalities.

- Covenant from sub-tenant direct with landlord to perform the covenants of the head-lease.

- Guarantee covenant from sub-tenant's guarantor.

- Time limit within which transaction is to be completed (typically three months).

Summary

The landlord is under a duty to notify its decision on an application for consent to assignment or sub-letting within a reasonable time, starting with the making of the application. To engage the duty, the application must have been served in accordance with the lease.

Time will run, once an application has been made, even though the tenant has supplied incomplete information, and possibly even though no security for costs has been provided.

Important factors in assessing whether the landlord has dealt with the application within a reasonable time may be the history of requests for, and provision of, relevant information, also any circumstances making the application particularly urgent for the tenant.

One way in which a landlord can relieve time pressure is to issue consent, subject to conditions designed to address outstanding matters of concern.

A potential difficulty for the landlord is that if it needs to avoid waiving a right to forfeit, that does not relieve it of its duties under the *Landlord and Tenant Act 1988*.

The landlord must state all its reasons fully, if refusing consent, or imposing conditions.

If consenting, it will require the consent to take the form of a formal licence deed, with appropriate terms and protections.

CHAPTER TEN
CONDUCT OF APPLICATIONS – ALTERATIONS; INFORMAL CONSENTS

This chapter considers the conduct of applications for landlord's consent to alterations, by both landlord and tenant. Like the previous chapter, it addresses the formalities for making an application, and the time constraints upon the landlord issuing its decision. The provisions of the *Alterations Protocol* are also discussed, together with the typical content of licence deeds.

This chapter also considers the difficulties in avoiding giving consent informally in correspondence; an issue common to all types of consent applications.

In contrast to the position in relation to alienation consents, there are relatively few constraints on the conduct of applications for consent to alterations.

Making the application

The general law imposes no formality for making an application for consent to alterations. The lease may contain provision governing the service of applications for consent, in which case of course the prescribed procedures should be followed. It is more likely that the lease will set out how notices should be served, but contain no provision which extends to the service of applications for consent.

The *Alterations Protocol* states that the application should be served in accordance with the terms of the lease, the meaning of which is slightly opaque in its application to circumstances where there is no lease provision governing service of *applications*. It may mean either (a) that there is no restriction, and that an application can be served in any way, so long as it comes to the attention of the landlord; or (b) that the provision relating to service of *notices* should be followed. The latter interpretation would equate the rule in the alterations context with that applied to alienation in *E.ON UK PLC v Gilesports Ltd [2012] 3 EGLR 23*.

The important difference in the case of alienation is that compliance with the service formalities is a statutory requirement. In the alterations context, by contrast, unless the lease contains a mandatory provision governing service of applications for consent, no adverse consequences flow from the application being made in a way which does not comply with the service provisions of the lease. That said, adopting those formalities should give greater certainty as to when the application is to be regarded as having been made, which may be important for the purposes of *s.3, Landlord and Tenant Act 1927* (see further below) as well as being useful if there is a dispute about unreasonable delay.

Time constraints on landlord

Lack of remedy for delay

When dealing with alterations, the *Landlord and Tenant Act 1988* does not apply. There is no statutory duty to give consent within a reasonable time. The statutory implied provision under *s.19(2), Landlord and Tenant Act 1927* is for consent not to be unreasonably withheld, with no mention of unreasonable delay. However, a delay for a sufficient period can amount to a withholding. An express lease provision may encompass unreasonable delay as well as withholding, of course. In any event there is no claim for damages against the landlord in the event that it does withhold consent unreasonably, or delay unreasonably (see chapter 2).

As a result, there is a dearth of authority on what might constitute a reasonable time for dealing with an application for consent to alterations. The *Alterations Protocol* does not list the factors which are likely to be relevant, by way of contrast to the *Alienation Protocol*. However, the matters listed there are equally likely to be relevant to the assessment of a reasonable time in relation to alterations.

The *Alterations Protocol* acknowledges that there is no statutory oblig-ation, and may be no obligation in the lease, for the landlord to respond within a reasonable time. However, it states that it is good practice for the landlord to do so, and notes that the response time may be relevant to costs in the event of subsequent dispute.

<u>Avoiding waiver of the right to forfeit</u>

As discussed in the previous chapter in relation to alienation, situations may arise where an application for consent to alterations is made, but the landlord needs to avoid waiving a right to forfeit the lease.

Tenants frequently effect alterations to premises without seeking consent. When the landlord discovers what has happened, the tenant then applies for retrospective consent. (The maxim that "*It is better to seek forgiveness than to ask for permission*" seems to command a high level of agreement among tenants, where alterations are concerned). The problem is much less difficult for the landlord who has an application for consent to alterations to respond to, than it is for the landlord faced with an application for consent to assignment or sub-letting. There is usually no requirement not to delay unreasonably, and no risk of having to pay damages in any event. Ultimately, though, a landlord who does not deal with the application for a sufficiently long period risks a finding that consent has been unreasonably withheld, so it is still an issue.

The nearest thing to a solution is the same as that identified in relation to alienation: make sure that all correspondence is 'without prejudice', and tie continuing consideration of the application to the possibility of an application for relief from forfeiture.

In passing, where a tenant has changed the use of the premises and seeks change-of-use consent retrospectively, there is no problem. Breach of user covenant is regarded as a continuing breach of covenant, so that a fresh right to forfeit arises after each act of waiver.

s.3, Landlord and Tenant Act 1927 – three-month time limit

There is often a quite separate and more easily identified time constraint, in circumstances where the tenant's application includes or constitutes service on the landlord of a notice under *s.3, Landlord and Tenant Act 1927*. The procedure under *s.3* provides a means for tenants to overcome their landlord's objections to alterations, and it will be considered in the next chapter. For now, the salient point is that service of a s.3 notice triggers a three-month period in which the landlord may respond. If the landlord fails to do so, then the tenant will be entitled to carry out the works referred to in the notice, whatever the lease may say. It is therefore a time limit that landlords should not lose sight of.

A peculiarity of the procedure under *s.3* is that there is no prescribed form of notice; all that is required is that the landlord should be notified of the tenant's intention to carry out the works, with a specification and plan showing the works and the part of the existing premises which would be affected. It is probable that a high proportion of applications for consent to alterations actually constitute notices under *s.3*, without either party being aware of it. It is prudent to assume that any application amounts to a s.3 notice, and to diarise the three-month deadline for a response.

Information required

As regards the information which should support the application, the *Alterations Protocol* provides that (as one would expect) the tenant should ensure that its application sufficiently describes the works, where appropriate by reference to detailed plans, drawings and specifications. The different considerations which the landlord may have in mind in relation to different categories of works were outlined in chapter 7. By way of reminder, the *Alterations Protocol* provides that the application should provide information to enable the landlord to identify:

- Whether the proposed alterations fall within the demise

- Whether the works are structural or non-structural

- What are the works for which consent is needed

- Whether there are any proposed works for which consent is not needed

- Which are the works (if any) which are subject to an absolute prohibition; and

- Which are the works (if any) which are subject to a provision that the landlord's consent cannot be unreasonably withheld.

It goes on to provide that when an application is received, the landlord should respond within five working days, confirming receipt, and either specifying what further information is needed, or explaining why more time is needed to identify what further information is going to be required.

Ideally within the same timescale, the landlord should pass on the application to any superior landlord whose consent will also be required.

Like the *Alienation Protocol*, it envisages that the tenant should aim to provide all relevant information in a single package. If further inform-ation is required, that should be the subject of a single request from the landlord, and the tenant should aim to provide all information so requested in a single package.

Costs

On the subject of costs, the *Alterations Protocol* indicates that a landlord will generally be reasonable to insist upon an undertaking as to costs, and states rather more confidently than does the *Alienation Protocol* that it will also generally be reasonable to suspend dealing with the application until one has been given.

The landlord's decision

Since the *Landlord and Tenant Act 1988* does not apply, there is no statutory duty to state reasons for the landlord's response, not is there any required formality as to how it is communicated.

The *Alterations Protocol* provides that the landlord's response to the tenant should be sufficiently detailed to enable the tenant to understand the landlord's position, and in particular that it should state whether the landlord:

- consents, and if so whether any conditions are attached to such consent;

- withholds its consent because it does not have sufficient information, and if so what further information it requires; or

- refuses its consent, and if so the reasons for such refusal.

It goes on to note the advisability of the landlord setting out its reasons fully, even though there is no requirement to do so. The landlord will be confined, in any subsequent litigation over the reasonableness of its decision, to reliance only upon those reasons which were actually in its mind at the time of the decision (*Tollbench Ltd v Plymouth City Council [1988] 1 EGLR 79*), and it will therefore benefit in evidential terms from having explained its reasons at the time.

Documenting the landlord's consent

As in the case of assignment or subletting, the landlord will generally want to have consent documented in a formal licence deed.

Typical provisions in a licence to alter might include:

- The tenant should supply the landlord with copies of all statutory permissions and approvals required.

- The appointment of any contractors by the tenant requires prior approval by the landlord.

- The works should be commenced within a specified time limit.

- Provision as to the manner in which the works are to be carried out, i.e. in compliance with applicable regulations, causing no nuisance to neighbours, in a good and workmanlike manner, etc..

- On completion, the tenant should notify the landlord, remove all debris and rubbish, and provide the landlord with relevant documentation such as the health and safety file for the works.

- An obligation to reinstate the works at lease expiry.

- Agreement of any guarantor.

Informal consents

This chapter has so far been concerned specifically with applications for consent to alterations; this section, though, is relevant to all types of consent application, but perhaps principally to alienation applications.

It should be apparent from the outlines given in this chapter and the last of the typical contents of formal licence deeds, in relation to the different types of consent, that as well as the simple 'yes' to the tenant's application, there is a variety of other matters which the landlord will wish to have addressed. Some are administrative, though important, and others such as guarantors' consents, and direct covenants, go to the commercial heart of the matter. It is crucial that consent be documented in a way which addresses these concerns adequately.

Some modern leases provide that unless consent is embodied in a formal licence deed, then no consent is given. This is ideal; unfortunately, it is far from universal. Where a lease simply refers to 'consent', with no further definition or regulation of what 'consent' is (other than, usually, a reference to consent being in writing), then consent may simply be the word 'yes', and of course that can be communicated informally in correspondence.

Problems have arisen where, although stopping short of saying 'yes', sufficient indications have been given in correspondence to amount to a communication of consent. Once consent has been given informally, the landlord may have difficulties in securing the terms and protections it wishes to see in a licence deed.

In *Aubergine Enterprises Ltd v Lakewood International Ltd [2002] EWCA Civ 177*, the landlord's agents wrote to the effect that the landlord "*would be prepared in principle to grant a licence for assignment of the lease*". The landlord solicitors subsequently wrote that the landlord "*had agreed in principle to grant a licence for assignment*". There followed lengthy and unsuccessful negotiations over the landlord's requirement for an undertaking as to costs, and other matters, which were never completely resolved. No formal licence deed was issued.

The assignee was in this case purchasing a long leasehold interest, and paying a considerable premium for it (£4.68 million). When the assignee encountered financial difficulties, it wished to evade this significant commitment if it could. After the completion date, its solicitors wrote purporting to rescind the contract on the basis that landlord's consent had not been obtained.

The court held that landlord's consent had been given in correspondence. The use of the qualification "*in principle*" did not prevent that correspondence amounting to a consent, nor did the fact that the relevant letters had been headed, in one case, 'subject to contract and without prejudice', and in the other 'subject to licence'. As regards the latter heading, the court held that it could not have had the effect of making consent subject to a formal licence deed, since the lease did not require that. There were outstanding landlord's requirements, expressed to be conditions of any consent, but the court found that a conditional consent was still a consent, even though the conditions might not have been fulfilled.

The purported rescission of the contract for want of landlord's consent was therefore of no effect. This is a case in which both sides accepted that the transaction would not proceed; there was no attempt to obtain specific performance, and the dispute was essentially about whether the assignee could recover the deposit, or whether it would be retained by the assignor. It gives no assistance, therefore, on the questions whether the parties could have been required to execute a formal licence deed, and if so what its terms might be.

The same issue arose on similar facts in *Alchemy Estates Ltd v Astor [2008] EWHC 2675 (Ch)*, where the assignee had purported to rescind in order to renegotiate the purchase price. The judge observed:

> "*Although the consent was expressed to be in principle and to be conditional upon the payment of reasonable costs and the execution and delivery of a formal licence to assign in the form of a deed, it is clear ... that a consent given subject to certain conditions may be sufficient...*"

The assignor in that case succeeded in obtaining an order for specific performance against the assignee. The licence deed had been executed by the landlord and the assignor, but not the assignee, though there were no outstanding issues on the form of the deed. It seems reasonable to assume that the detail of the order for specific performance would have included an order requiring the assignee to execute the licence deed, though the report is silent as to this point.

In *Next plc v NFU Mutual Insurance [1997] EGCS 181*, taken in the context of the surrounding circumstances and correspondence, the 'consent' consisted of a letter headed 'subject to licence' containing the words "*I have now instructed our solicitors to issue a draft licence*", followed by the submission of a draft.

There the tenants sought, not only a declaration that landlord's consent had been granted, but also an injunction requiring the landlord to execute the licence in the form which had been agreed. The outcome was therefore not that the landlords failed to secure the required licence, but that they could not prevent the assignment. Their objection was that information had emerged very late in the day casting serious doubt over the assignee's financial position. In normal circumstances, of course, that would be a legitimate reason for refusal of consent, but in this instance it was too late. They had already consented.

This problem can sometimes occur where the tenant has been exerting acute pressure to obtain the landlord's consent, and threatening court action. To relieve the pressure, once the landlord has decided that it will consent, its advisors may use expressions such as "*consents in principle*", "*is minded to consent*", "*will consent*", or "*is prepared to consent*". Although everything depends upon construction in the particular context, the risk (indeed the likelihood) is that a court would read that as meaning simply "*my client consents*". As appears from the above caselaw, headings such as 'subject to contract' or 'subject to licence' cannot be relied upon to give protection.

It is relatively unusual for a simple unconditional consent to be given. Usually consent will be conditional. *s.1(3)* of the 1988 Act contemplates a landlord doing only one of three things: (a) consenting, (b) withholding consent, or (c) consenting subject to conditions. On the basis of the caselaw just discussed, a landlord who has consented subject to conditions is quite simply a landlord who has consented.

It is not easy to identify an approach for landlords and their advisors which will reliably safeguard against this problem. Despite the caselaw, there is still potential usefulness in heading all letters 'subject to formal licence deed', and also stating in at least the initial letter acknowledging the application, if not in all letters, that consent will only be given when a formal licence deed has been executed. These forms of words help to build a picture of a landlord which continues to reserve its decision. In any event, little harm can come of using them, while the position will be even more difficult if they are absent.

Once the decision has been taken to allow the transaction to proceed, it is obviously important to avoid any form of words which indicates consent. *"We enclose a draft licence deed for consideration"* should be the most that is said. (The covering letter, of course, must give reasons for any conditions set out in the draft deed). On the strength of *Next plc v NFU Mutual Assurance*, even that may not be sufficient protection; though, if it is not, it is difficult to see how a landlord could ever avoid an informal consent.

The answer lies in the lease drafting, and landlords should ensure that their leases provide that a formal licence deed is the only means by which consent can be given.

Summary

There are no formal requirements for the way in which an application for consent to alterations is served.

There is no statutory requirement to make a decision within a reasonable time, though there may be a contractual one – even if there is, breach of it will not entitle the tenant to claim damages.

The three-month time limit for responding to a notice under *s.3, Landlord and Tenant Act 1927* means that it is prudent for landlords to aim to respond within three months, since many applications for consent to alterations are actually s.3 notices.

There are no formal requirements for stating reasons when making a decision on alterations, though it is useful for a landlord to have done so.

If consenting, the landlord will require the consent to take the form of a formal licence deed, with appropriate terms and protections.

Informal consents – all types of consent application

- Where correspondence from or on behalf of the landlord contains sufficient indications of consent, this may be held by the court to amount to a consent sufficient to satisfy the lease. That will effectively remove any incentive for tenants, guarantors and other parties to enter into a formal licence deed with the landlord, containing all the protections and ancillary terms which the landlord requires.

- Decided cases have held that headings such as 'subject to contract' or 'subject to licence' did not protect the landlord against having given consent in correspondence. The most important safeguard is not to use wording indicating consent.

- Ideally, leases should stipulate that consent can only be given in the form of a licence deed.

CHAPTER ELEVEN
OVERCOMING THE LANDLORD'S OBJECTIONS, AND REMEDIES WHERE THE LANDLORD IS UNREASONABLE

This chapter outlines the course of action available to a tenant where the landlord objects to an application. It considers the claim for damages under the Landlord and Tenant Act 1988, including the possibility of an award of exemplary damages, and the relevance of causation when considering combined applications. It goes on to discuss the other options of a claim for declaratory relief, or simply proceeding without landlord's consent. Finally, additional remedies relating specifically to alterations are outlined: modification/discharge of covenants under *s.84, Law of Property Act 1925*; *Sched 21, Equality Act 2010*; and *s.3* and *s.1, Landlord and Tenant Act 1927*.

The law gives tenants a range of weapons for use in a situation where a landlord is being unreasonable. What weapons the tenant chooses to deploy depend upon the circumstances, and what it is trying to achieve.

Prior to the *Landlord and Tenant Act 1988*, the conventional remedy in any case where the tenant was aggrieved by a landlord's withholding of consent was to apply to court for a declaration that the landlord's behaviour was unreasonable. Obtaining a declaration would take as long as any other type of litigation, and the delay could render this an ineffective remedy, certainly in the case of an assignment or sub-letting, where the third party might lose interest in the transaction and find alternative premises.

If a tenant is trying to obtain consent for alterations, though, the timing is unlikely to be as critical. The objective is quite simply to be able to do the work. A claim for a declaration may therefore be a useful way forward (and in any event a claim for damages is of course not available). Alternatively, a tenant who is confident in its judgment that the landlord is being unreasonable may decide simply to proceed with the works without consent. In this specific context of alterations, there are potentially other statutory routes to overcoming the landlord's resistance, which will be discussed later.

As regards an assignment or a sub-letting, the big difference is that a claim for damages is available. It is also possible, as in the case of alterations, for the tenant simply to go ahead with the transaction anyway, or to seek a declaration from the court. The first of those options depends upon the third party being willing to proceed on that basis, and the second may be thought only to be useful where the third party is still interested in the transaction. Where the transaction has fallen through because the third party has walked away from it, a claim for damages is the most obviously useful remedy, and in that case the objective will have switched from completion of the transaction, to obtaining compensation.

In fact, the tenant may sensibly seek both a declaration and damages, whether or not the third party is still interested. Proceedings will probably be issued at a time when they are, and if that is still the case when a declaration is obtained, the transaction can then safely go ahead. If damages were included in the claim, then as and when the third party does lose interest, there is no need for amendment of the claim or further case management directions on evidence. Nor is there any need to abandon the declaration element of the claim, which is still potentially useful in two ways. First, a declaration as to the landlord having behaved unreasonably on one occasion may be useful in the event of a subsequent application running into landlord's opposition. Secondly, it is always possible that the third party may still be looking for premises by the time the declaration is obtained, in which case it may be possible to revive the deal.

Our consideration of the available courses of action begins with a claim for damages.

Damages

General principle

Damages for a landlord's unreasonable withholding of consent, or unreasonable delay, are of course only available under the *Landlord and Tenant Act 1988*, and only in relation to consent for assignment, subletting, charging or parting with possession.

We have previously noted the possibility that damages for unreasonable delay could in theory be available even where landlord's consent is ultimately given. Also, as just described, a claim for damages may usefully be included in any proceedings even though the third party remains, for the time being, prepared to go ahead with the transaction. The applicability of the remedy is not therefore confined to situations where the transaction has failed. A threat to claim damages under the 1988 Act is something which a landlord will usually take seriously, and is one of the main ways of applying pressure on the landlord to give its consent.

The key issue in considering a claim for damages is of course 'how much'? What amount of damages will be recoverable? Although the claim is ultimately founded upon a contractual term (express or implied), *s.4* provides that the claim for damages under the 1988 Act is a *"claim in tort for breach of statutory duty"*. The aim of the award is therefore not that of a contractual damages award, to put the tenant into the position it would have been in had the contract been performed; but rather to put the tenant into the position it would have been in but for the landlord's breach of statutory duty.

Example: Design Progression v Thurloe Properties

How this will work out in practice must inevitably be fact-dependent, but the decision in *Design Progression Ltd v Thurloe Properties Ltd [2004] EWHC 324 (Ch)* provides a good basis for discussion of the factors which may often arise in a calculation of damages under the 1988 Act.

This was a case where the assignment was originally proposed in 2002, just over two years before lease expiry. The trial was heard in 2004, only two months before lease expiry. The tenant had stripped out the premises in early 2002 in anticipation of relocating, at a cost of £7,725. That cost did not form part of the recoverable damages, since it was incurred as a result of the decision to relocate, and not caused by any breach of duty by the landlord. The same applied to the tenant's solicitor's costs.

The tenant then reoccupied the premises from June 2002, a decision which the judge found to be unarguably reasonable. The premises were refitted for that purpose at a cost of £15,611.50, which was in principle recoverable. Upon vacating the premises at lease expiry, however, the tenant would have the value of most of the fittings, which it would be entitled to remove. Having little evidence as to what that value might be, the judge reduced this head of claim only slightly, to £14,000 plus VAT.

Had the landlord not been unreasonable, the premises would have been occupied by the assignee instead of left vacant before the tenant's reoccupation, and the assignee would have been responsible for the rent for that period, which was approximately one quarter. The tenant was entitled to claim the appropriate amount of the rent (the precise figure is not given in the judgment, but can be roughly calculated to be £30,000).

The tenant was moreover entitled to a figure for loss of turnover and goodwill incurred as a result of the temporary relocation, which was agreed to be £22,500.

Finally, it was a term of the failed deal that the tenant would receive a premium of £75,000, which was lost as a result of the landlord being unreasonable. Given the proximity to the end of the term, it was reasonable of the tenant not to have re-marketed, and so the court rejected the landlord's argument that there should be no damages recoverable under this head because the tenant retained beneficial use of the asset. The amount of the lost premium was also recoverable.

The calculation of damages in that case was untypical, because of the tenant having reoccupied. That had two consequences: (a) the costs of their refit came into account: and (b) the wasted rent element of the claim was limited, to the time from the expiry of the reasonable time for the landlord to have consented, up to the tenant going back into occupation. In a case where the tenant does not reoccupy, it is likely to be able to recover rent and outgoings up to the time when it has successfully assigned (or sub-let), or can reasonably expect to have done so.

Another untypical feature was that the failed transaction was so close to lease expiry, making it a sensible option for them to mitigate their loss by reoccupying, rather than remarketing. A tenant who remarkets may expect to have to take into account the benefit of the deal they do, or can expect to do, in future. So for example, if the evidence showed that on an assignment in future the tenant could expect to receive a premium of £50,000, that would have to be set against the £75,000 premium lost as a result of the landlord's unreasonableness. On the other hand, had another deal been concluded, the tenant could have expected to recover the solicitor's costs thrown away on the failed deal, since the landlord's breach of duty would have caused them to incur two sets of costs instead of just one.

Exemplary damages

In *Mount Eden Land Ltd v Folia Ltd [2003] EWHC 1815 (Ch)* the judge, Peter Smith J, raised the possibility of an award of exemplary or punitive damages in cases where a landlord has behaved particularly badly. In passing, it may have been observed how often the names Mount Eden Land Ltd and Mount Cook Land Ltd have appeared in the caselaw we have considered. The two companies are in common ownership, and have considerable landholdings in central London. Their robust attitude to tenants' applications for consent has seen them in court on numerous occasions, and they have received their share of adverse judicial comment. Be that as it may, exemplary damages were not awarded against them in that case, but it was Peter Smith J who also decided *Design Progression v Thurloe Properties*, and he returned to the theme there.

He observed:

> "*An award of exemplary damages is available where there is unacceptable behaviour on the part of the Defendant, and that behaviour displays features which merit punishment, where the Defendant acts in a way calculated to make a profit for himself which might well exceed the compensation payable to a Claimant.*"

Concluding that this was such a case, he said:

> "*It is clear in my judgment that the Defendant through its agents operated in a cynical way designed to frustrate the Claimant in obtaining its legitimate expectation namely an assignment of the premises coupled with a receipt of the £75,000 premium and an ending of its further obligations under the Lease. It was done to extract for itself the value of the property by virtue of the difference between the passing rent and the market rent when it had no legitimate reason for acting the way it did in response to the Claimant's application for licence to assign.*"

The award of exemplary damages in the case was in the sum of £25,000. The two passages quoted are sufficiently explicit as to the sort of circumstances in which such an award may be made.

Including the exemplary damages, the total award in *Design Progression v Thurloe Properties* was in the order of £166,500, to which must be added interest at 8% over two years, amounting to an additional £27,000 in round figures. With, presumably, both sides' costs to be added, the episode was an expensive one for the landlord, and illustrates why a threat of a damages claim does exert real pressure on landlords.

Combined applications and causation issues

It has been remarked previously that tactical considerations arise when an application for consent to assignment or sub-letting is coupled with other applications for consent to alteration and/or change of use. That this circumstance can have consequences for the tenant's damages claim is illustrated by *Clinton Cards (Essex) v Sun Alliance and London Assurance [2002] EWHC 1576 (Ch)*. In that case, a landlord refused consent to (a) a proposed sub-letting, and (b) an associated proposed change of use. As a result, the proposed transaction was lost. Both refusals were found to be unreasonable.

No damages are recoverable, of course, for unreasonable refusal of consent to change of use. The surprising feature of the case is that the tenant did not recover damages under the 1988 Act, in relation to the refusal of consent to the sub-letting. The court was persuaded that, had the landlord maintained only its wrongful refusal to the change of use, the sub-letting would have been prevented by that, regardless of the outcome of the application for consent to the sub-letting itself. It was therefore the change of use refusal which caused the tenant's loss.

It is not inevitable that there will be a similar outcome in any case where there are combined applications. The court will reach a conclusion on the causation aspects upon the evidence in the particular case. It is a cautionary tale, though, reminding one to be alive to issues of causation in such circumstances before commencing a damages claim. It also underlines how landlords may have more control over alienation than appears to be the case. The landlord's strategy in the case was actually a high-risk one; it would have been safer to consent to the sub-letting, but refuse consent to the change of use. No claim for damages could then have been entertained.

Declaratory relief

The usual claim is for declarations (a) that consent has been unreasonably withheld or delayed (or made subject to unreasonable conditions), and (b) that the tenant is entitled to proceed with the alterations/assignment/sub-letting without any further act of consent from the landlord.

Armed with those declarations, the tenant can proceed without any fear of enforcement action by the landlord. Care must be taken, though, not to step outside the bounds of the action for which consent has been requested, since it will be the landlord's refusal of consent to that specific action which is the subject of the declaration. In the case of a sub-letting, for example, where the landlord has been provided with a copy of the form of proposed sub-lease, and has been declared to have been unreasonable in withholding consent to it, the tenant should be very wary of agreeing with the sub-tenant anything but the most minor administrative changes to the document.

As regards alterations, although a declaration will enable the tenant to go ahead with its works, there is a potential consequence on rent review. While rent review clauses will invariably provide that alterations carried out at the tenant's expense are not to be valued, leases increasingly have an exception from that in the case of alterations carried out without the landlord's consent. Even if the landlord is declared to have unreasonably withheld consent, a tenant who carries out the alterations accordingly may find that it pays a higher rent upon review. This point applies also where the tenant simply proceeds with the work without obtaining a declaration, and where the work is done pursuant to a court authorisation under *s.3, Landlord and Tenant Act 1927* (dealt with later in this chapter).

Proceeding without either consent or declaration

It may be recalled from chapter 2 that (except where the *Landlord and Tenant Act 1988* applies) the function of a proviso for landlord's consent not to be unreasonably withheld is not to give the tenant a cause of action, but to provide a defence. In other words, if (a) a tenant seeks consent to do something which requires landlord's consent; (b) the landlord unreasonably refuses it; and (c) the tenant then goes ahead and does it anyway, the presence of the proviso establishes that there is no breach of covenant on the tenant's part.

A robust-minded tenant may therefore take the view that it does not need to spend time and money getting a declaration from the court, but can simply go ahead. This has been confirmed as lawful in the alien-

ation context (*Treloar v Bigge (1874) LR 9 Ex 151*), and also for alterations (*Old Grovebury Manor Farm Ltd v Seymour Plant Sales and Hire
Ltd (No. 2) [1979] 1 WLR 1397*).

There are obvious risks in this course, since the landlord's refusal of
consent may subsequently be found to have been reasonable. In that
case the tenant will have been in breach of covenant. That gives rise to a
risk of forfeiture, and while that might be welcome to a tenant whose
aim was to bring to an end its lease commitment, it will be a serious
problem for an assignee or sub-tenant. The next chapter considers the
actions open to a landlord where the tenant has proceeded without
consent.

For a tenant who is minded to go down this route, it is usually the prospect of the landlord forfeiting the lease by peaceable re-entry which is
the biggest potential problem. The cost and disruption of defending
court proceedings can be anticipated and budgeted for, but turning up
in the morning to find the locks have been changed is a different matter
entirely. Apart from disruption and reputational damage, the tenant is
immediately on the back foot, and must drop everything to work with
lawyers in making a claim for relief from forfeiture, and obtaining an
interim injunction to restore them to occupation pending the determination of the application for relief. Potentially this can be pre-empted by
asking the landlord to confirm that any forfeiture will be effected by
court proceedings rather than peaceable re-entry, and by obtaining an
injunction to restrict the landlord to forfeiture by court proceedings if
the confirmation is not forthcoming.

In practice, in the case of assignment or sub-letting it is difficult to
proceed in this way for the simple reason that the prospective assignee
or sub-tenant is unlikely to take the risk. If they can be persuaded to do
so, they will invariably require to be indemnified against any loss by the
tenant.

Alterations – specific measures

There are three statutory routes to overcoming a landlord's objections to proposed alterations. The one which is of the widest application and most usefulness is that under *s.3, Landlord and Tenant Act 1927*. The other two options will be addressed first.

Modification or discharge of alterations covenant

When freehold land is subject to a restrictive covenant, application can be made to the Lands Chamber of the Upper Tribunal under *s.84, Law of Property Act 1925*, to discharge or modify the restriction. That is a familiar jurisdiction; it is perhaps not so well-known that the jurisdiction extends to restrictive covenants in leases, although only to long leases. That is, the lease must have been granted for more than 40 years, and at least 25 years must have already expired (*s.84(12)*). Application may be made in relation to any restrictive covenant in a lease, and not just covenants relating to alterations.

To succeed, the tenant would have to satisfy one of the four available grounds under *s.84*, which are the same as those for the modification or discharge of freehold covenants:

(a) Changes in the character of the property or the neighbourhood or other circumstances mean that the restriction ought to be deemed obsolete. Reliance on this ground is rarely successful, and including it in the application can lead to adverse costs consequences.

(aa) The continued existence of the covenant would impede some reasonable user. This ground only applies where the Tribunal is also satisfied that the restriction:

   • Does not secure any practical benefit of substantial value or advantage to those with the benefit; or

- Is contrary to the public interest (this ground rarely applies – *Re Collins Application (1975) 30 P&CR 527* at *531*);

- And in either case, that money will be an adequate compensation.

(b) Those with the benefit of the restriction have agreed to the modification or discharge.

(c) Modification or discharge will not injure the persons entitled to the benefit of the restriction.

The Tribunal has a discretion even where one or more of the substantive grounds are established.

Difficulties of proving the statutory grounds, and the restriction to leases of over 40 years in length, mean that this option is little-used, but situations can and do arise when it offers a useful way forward.

Schedule 21, Equality Act 2010

Specific provisions concerning landlords' consent apply where the alterations are proposed in order to comply with the duty to make reasonable adjustments for disabled persons under the *Equality Act 2010*. *s.20* of the 2010 Act defines the duty to make reasonable adjustments as comprising three requirements. For present purposes the relevant one is

"a requirement, where a physical feature puts a disabled person at a substantial disadvantage in relation to a relevant matter in comparison with persons who are not disabled, to take such steps as it is reasonable to have to take to avoid the disadvantage."

Those subject to the duty are: service-providers; employers; education providers; and members' associations. Those categories will catch many commercial occupiers.

Schedule 21 applies where the person to whom the duty applies is a tenant, who is not "*entitled to make the alterations*". Four situations are envisaged by that expression:

- the lease prohibits the alterations absolutely;

- the landlord has refused consent,

- the lease imposes conditions on the consent, or

- the landlord has imposed conditions on the consent.

In these circumstances, regardless of the actual terms of the lease, the tenancy has effect as if:

- The tenant can make the alteration with the landlord's written consent.

- The tenant must make a written application for consent.

- The landlord must not unreasonably withhold consent, but can grant consent subject to reasonable conditions.

If the landlord refuses to give consent, or imposes a condition on the consent, the tenant or a disabled person with an interest in the alter-ation being made can refer the matter to a county court, for a determination as to whether the refusal or condition is unreasonable. Where it is a disabled person who is bringing an action against the tenant under the reasonable adjustment duty, *Schedule 21* also provides for a landlord to be joined as a party to the proceedings.

The *Equality Act 2010 (Disability) Regulations 2010 (SI 2010/2128)* provide more detail on how this regime works. *Regulations 10-14* set out five circumstances where the landlord will be deemed to have withheld consent (and therefore the matter can be referred to the county court):

- The landlord has neither given nor refused consent within 42 days from the date it receives from the tenant a full written application for consent (with reasonable plans and specifications in support).

- The landlord thinks the written application for consent lacks plans and specifications which it is reasonable to require, but fails to request the missing items from the tenant within 21 days of receipt of the application for consent.

- The landlord fails to give or refuse consent to the alterations within a further period of 42 days from receipt of the missing plans and specifications.

- The landlord gives consent within 42 days, conditionally upon receiving consent from a superior landlord (or other party), but the landlord does not, within the 42-day period, apply in writing for that superior consent (with all the supporting plans and specifications). The application for superior consent must make it clear that the tenant wishes to alter the premises in order to comply with its duty to make reasonable adjustments under the *Equality Act 2010*, and that the landlord has given consent conditionally on the other party consenting.

- The landlord fails to inform the tenant that it has received the superior consent within 14 days of receiving it.

The regime thus provides a fairly comprehensive statutory framework within which a tenant can establish entitlement to carry out its proposed works, and it is to be noted that this procedure may override even an absolute prohibition in the lease.

Although it is a potentially useful structure, it is fair to say that it is not in day-to-day use. First, its applicability is restricted to commercial tenants falling within the classes to whom the duty applies, and to adjustments for disabled persons. Secondly, it ultimately boils down to the familiar issue of reasonableness, and so adds little to the general law. Thirdly, it is unusual for a landlord to have any serious objection to disability adjustment works: even if the landlord is not particularly altruistic, the potential for reputational damage as a result of objecting is significant, and a property that does not benefit from such adjustments may command lower rents than other properties that do.

s.3, Landlord and Tenant Act 1927

While the two statutory regimes discussed so far are of limited applicability, s.3 has wide general application. As suggested in the previous chapter, it is entirely likely that many applications for consent to alterations constitute notices under s.3, although the parties may be unaware of this.

s.3 applies to leases of property used for a trade or business, with the exceptions of mining leases and some agricultural leases. Contracting-out is not possible. A tenant may want to use the procedure even if it is thought that landlord's consent will not be problematic, because s.3 can bring with it a right to compensation.

Like s.19(2) of the 1927 Act, s.3 refers to 'improvements', but can be read as meaning 'alterations'. A tenant who proposes to carry out improvements can serve a notice on the landlord to that effect. There is no prescribed form, but it must be accompanied by a plan and specification which shows the improvements and the part of the property affected by them, in sufficient detail to enable the landlord to reach a decision. Ideally the notice would also make it clear that the tenant is intending to exercise its rights under s.3, although a specific reference to a future claim for compensation may not be necessary (*Deerfield Travel Services Limited v Leathersellers Company (1983) 46 P&CR 132*).

If the landlord does not object to the improvements within three months then the tenant may lawfully carry them out, even if the lease would prohibit this.

Instead of objecting to the works, a landlord can offer to do them itself in return for a reasonable increase in the rent (determined by the county court if not agreed). A tenant is under no obligation to accept this offer and may withdraw its notice. If it does so, the landlord then has no right to carry out the works and increase the rent. Equally the tenant cannot carry out the works, having withdrawn its notice, so the result may be an unsatisfactory stalemate.

If the landlord does object, then the likelihood is that the parties would negotiate the application and try to agree terms which will deal with the landlord's objections. Should a negotiated solution be impossible, the tenant has the right to apply to the court for authorisation to carry out the improvements. The court can authorise the improvements if they:

- Are calculated to add to the letting value of the property at the termination of the tenancy (this factor is not relevant to whether the work qualifies as an 'improvement' within the meaning of the Act, but is a pre-condition of authorisation of the works against the landlord's objections);

- Are reasonable and suitable to the character of the property;

- Will not diminish the value of any other property which belongs to the landlord or to any superior landlord.

The court may modify the plans and specification of the works and impose conditions as it thinks fit.

Like the procedures under s.84, *Law of Property Act 1925*, and the *Equality Act 2010*, this route offers the ability to overcome even an absolute prohibition in the lease.

After completing the works, the tenant should apply to the landlord for a certificate that the works have been duly executed pursuant to s.3. If the landlord fails to give this certificate within one month, or refuses to give it, then the tenant can apply to the court for a certificate. If the tenant is to claim compensation at the end of the term, this certificate is evidentially useful.

The right to compensation for improvements at the end of the term is set out in *s.1* of the 1927 Act. Consideration of the nature of the claim falls outside the scope of this book, but it may be observed that a claim for under *s.1* is a rarity, for a number of reasons. However, the right to claim can often assist a tenant in negotiating down a dilapidations claim.

Summary

Damages for a landlord's breach of the statutory duties under the *Landlord and Tenant Act 1988* are assessed on a tortious basis. What heads of damages will be recoverable is fact-dependent, but typical heads of claim might include:

- Rent payable from the date of the landlord's unreasonable withholding of consent, up to the time when the tenant has concluded a new assignment or sub-letting, or could reasonably expect to have done so.

- Solicitor's costs thrown away on the failed deal.

- Any lost premium which would have been paid as part of the failed deal, after making allowance for any premium which has been, or could be expected to be, achieved on a new deal.

Where the landlord's behaviour is thought to have been such as to merit punishment, and designed to make a profit in excess of the compensation payable to the tenant, the court may mark its disapproval by an award of exemplary or punitive damages.

A court may conclude that no damages are payable where the unreasonable withholding of consent to assignment or sub-letting has not been causative of the loss, for example where refusal of consent to an associated application for consent to change of use is what caused the third party to abandon the deal.

Where timing allows, or where a claim for damages is unavailable because the *Landlord and Tenant Act 1988* does not apply, an alternative is to apply to court for declaratory relief. If successful, that enables the tenant to proceed with its proposed action without being in breach of covenant.

A claim for a declaration is often combined with a claim for damages under the 1988 Act, regardless of whether the deal has failed.

A tenant who is sure of its ground may omit to apply for a declaration, and simply go ahead without consent. If they are right, that the landlord is unreasonable, then there is no breach of covenant. The risk is that they are wrong, and then they will be exposed to enforcement action by the landlord.

As regards alterations, a landlord's objections can potentially be overcome (even where the alterations are absolutely prohibited under the lease) using one of three statutory procedures:

- Under *s.84, Law of Property Act 1925*, application can be made to modify or discharge the alterations covenant, though only in the case of leases granted for over 40 years, where at least 25 years of the term have elapsed.

- Under the *Equality Act 2010*, where an occupier is under the statutory duty to make reasonable adjustments to premises for disabled persons, but is not entitled to do so under the lease, the county court can effectively authorise the works.

- Under *s.3, Landlord and Tenant Act 1927*, the county court can authorise works which will add to the letting value of the premises at lease expiry.

MORE BOOKS BY
LAW BRIEF PUBLISHING

A selection of our other titles available now:-

'A Practical Guide to Immigration Law and Tier 1 Entrepreneur Applications' by Sarah Pinder
'A Practical Guide to Unlawful Eviction and Harassment' by Stephanie Lovegrove
'In My Backyard! A Practical Guide to Neighbourhood Plans' by Dr Sue Chadwick
'A Practical Guide to the Law Relating to Food' by Ian Thomas
'A Practical Guide to the Ending of Assured Shorthold Tenancies' by Elizabeth Dwomoh
'Commercial Mediation – A Practical Guide' by Nick Carr
'A Practical Guide to Financial Services Claims' by Chris Hegarty
'The Law of Houses in Multiple Occupation: A Practical Guide to HMO Proceedings' by Julian Hunt
'A Practical Guide to Unlawful Eviction and Harassment' by Stephanie Lovegrove
'A Practical Guide to Solicitor and Client Costs' by Robin Dunne
'Artificial Intelligence – The Practical Legal Issues' by John Buyers
'A Practical Guide to Wrongful Conception, Wrongful Birth and Wrongful Life Claims' by Rebecca Greenstreet
'Occupiers, Highways and Defective Premises Claims: A Practical Guide Post-Jackson – 2nd Edition' by Andrew Mckie
'A Practical Guide to Financial Ombudsman Service Claims' by Adam Temple & Robert Scrivenor
'A Practical Guide to the Law of Enfranchisement and Lease Extension' by Paul Sams
'A Practical Guide to Marketing for Lawyers – 2nd Edition' by Catherine Bailey & Jennet Ingram
'A Practical Guide to Advising Schools on Employment Law' by Jonathan Holden

'The Queen's Counsel Lawyer's Omnibus: 20 Years of Cartoons from The Times 1993-2013' by Alex Steuart Williams

These books and more are available to order online direct from the publisher at www.lawbriefpublishing.com, where you can also read free sample chapters. For any queries, contact us on 0844 587 2383 or mail@lawbriefpublishing.com.

Our books are also usually in stock at www.amazon.co.uk with free next day delivery for Prime members, and at good legal bookshops such as Hammicks and Wildy & Sons.

We are regularly launching new books in our series of practical day-to-day practitioners' guides. Visit our website and join our free newsletter to be kept informed and to receive special offers, free chapters, etc.

You can also follow us on Twitter at www.twitter.com/lawbriefpub.